LITTLE SHIP NAVIGATION

PLATE I

Plate   I. "Mini" Hand Bearing Compass

LITTLE SHIP
NAVIGATION

By

M. J. RANTZEN
Lieut.-Commr. (Sp), R.N.V.R.
Hon. Navigation Instructor, Little Ship Club, 1945–1975

Illustrated by M. A. Moffat

BARRIE & JENKINS
COMMUNICA-EUROPA

© *Copyright*, 1970, 1973, 1977
M. J. Rantzen
First published by
Herbert Jenkins Ltd.
1949
Reprinted 1956, 1961
2nd edition 1964
Fifth impression 1970
Sixth impression 1973
3rd edition 1977
Published by Barrie & Jenkins Ltd.
24 Highbury Crescent
London N5 1RX

ISBN 0 214 20374 3

Made and printed in Great Britain by
A. Wheaton & Co., Exeter.

FOREWORD TO THE FIRST EDITION

By CAPTAIN A. HOPWOOD, Extra Master (Ord.)

Late Senior Examiner, Masters and Mates, London

When I was asked by the Author to accept the dedication of this book and write a Foreword to it, I accepted in the belief that the offer was not only a compliment to myself but also to the profession to which I have the honour to belong.

My association with little ship men has been in the past more of an official than a personal character, and in my capacity as an Examiner I learned much about the men themselves, their diverse interests, and of the difficulties which confront them in their quest for nautical knowledge and experience.

The purpose of a Foreword, as I understand it, is not to confuse the reader with additional rules and maxims, but rather to direct his attention to the contents of the book and emphasise if possible their value to him.

With the knowledge that my practical training has been largely gained seaward of the five-fathom line, I am a little apprehensive of the effect that any remarks that I as a professional seaman may make, will have on the men who do most of their sailing between that invisible boundary and what is commonly called the shore.

Viewing these contrasting conditions objectively, however, my conclusions are that many of the practices of navigators are common to big and little ships alike when cruising in coastal waters and only diverge when a course is set for the wider oceans.

"Safety first" is the common aim of both, and to ensure this a methodical use of all available navigational aids is essential.

Reliance on judgment alone is guesswork, and to persist in this crude method of fixing positions and distances when other means are at hand is a gamble, ultimately ending in loss of life and property.

Having read with interest the introductory remarks of the Author and the eighteen chapters which follow, I have formed the opinion that the little ship men are fortunate to have within their reach so many useful data applicable to their needs within one cover.

Skilfully compiled from his own experiences of the requirements of little ship navigators, it exposes the fallacy of rule-of-thumb and presents a clear, common-sense picture of coastal navigation without tears.

All the problems which are likely to puzzle the beginner are dealt with at length, and taken as a whole the book constitutes a concise epitome of navigational theories and practices sufficient for little ship men to extract the maximum amount of pleasure from limited cruises with a minimum of anxiety or even danger.

It is not my intention here to discuss the technical details involved or weigh up the merits of one method against another. This has been amply dealt with in the text, and the reader having mastered the facts will choose for himself.

Some reference, however, to the fundamentals of coastal navigation may not be out of place and should be of interest to all little ship men.

Legends and near-legends of the sea are numerous and often amusing. but one that has stood the test of time and should be taken seriously is that of the three L's, Lead, Log and Lookout. Although scientific research has discovered speedier and less onerous methods of obtaining the same results, little ship men are obliged to use them in their simple and original forms.

Nautical history recalls numerous examples of over-confidence or ignorance delaying the use of one or all of these safeguards, disaster following swiftly in the wake of this neglect.

The Author has knowledgeably devoted a chapter to the maintenance and use of this equipment. Careful study of it will repay the beginner and doubtless the legend will be passed on to the next generation.

Accuracy in position finding and plotting should be desired

by all navigators.   For this to be accomplished satisfactorily a reasonable proficiency in the use of the navigational instruments required for the purpose is essential.

Navigational instruments are the tools of the trade, and as in other spheres amateurs have proved themselves as skilful as professionals, no reason exists why initial difficulties, seemingly unsurmountable by beginners, should not by practice be readily overcome and proficiency attained.   The Author has devoted considerable space to this subject, clearing up anomalies so that confidence may be placed in results.

Under the title of " Planning " an interesting feature associated with coastal navigation is introduced.   Where time-saving and prudent finance are factors for consideration, it is imperative ; but in any circumstances every effort should be made to adopt method and foresight.

Without local knowledge—which includes buoyage systems, landmarks, etc.—and tidal information, plans cannot be formulated.   From charts of the area through which it is intended to pass much of the required data will be found which can be readily amplified by reference to official publications. Few beginners are unfamilar with the simple phenomena of tides, but if full advantage is to be taken of their ebb and flow—and the effect can be considerable—a further study of this subject will assist in planning more ambitious enterprises with fewer possibilities of failure.

A special feature of this volume is the collection of illus-trations and diagrams carefully chosen and executed, amply fulfilling the role for which they are intended.

In concluding this Foreword I offer a word of encouragement to all beginners and, indeed, to a somewhat wider public.

Expert navigators are not made in a day, and like their professional counterparts little ship men will gain confidence with added knowledge and experience when these are based on sound principles.

I commend this book to all who are interested in the art and are desirous of acquiring those principles.

A. H.

PREFACE TO THE THIRD EDITION
(Plus a practical tip)

This book, which first appeared in 1949, and the first two editions of which served as text books for the regular courses of lectures in Coastal Navigation given by the author as Honorary Navigation Instructor to the Little Ship Club over a period of thirty years, was written to meet the special needs of yachtsmen, that is to say, of the masters of little ships which go to sea for pleasure. No other shipmaster is more dependent upon careful and accurate navigation, for no other class of ship is more affected by the uncontrollable movements of the sea she rides. Yet it is still true that no other class of shipmaster is more prone to slipshod navigation by methods of such inaccuracy that no professional navigator would tolerate them.

The master of the little ship is essentially an amateur. His time at sea is all too limited: his time for preliminary study even more so. He is usually neither mathematically minded nor mathematically trained, and although he is both willing and able to learn, the admirable but formidable tomes from which the professional navigator learns his trade are not for him. His need is for instruction which is practical rather than academic and is presented in a form suited to one whose sea-going is a spare time occupation, but which nevertheless teaches methods which are acceptable by professional standards; for the well-tried practices of those who spend their lives at sea should be followed wherever possible. It is still the cardinal fault of much navigation instruction and of many "yachtsmen's" navigation books that, in order to achieve a simplicity that is apparent rather than real, they all too lightly discard "official" methods in favour of methods which are, at best, inaccurate and at worst positively dangerous, as many a yachtsman has found to his cost.

The gratifying way in which this work has become accepted as a standard text book by English-speaking little ship masters all over the World during nearly three decades of published life provides renewed proof, if proof be needed, of the correctness of the proposition that simplicity and accuracy should go hand in hand without sacrifice of the latter to the former. This is the reason why this third edition, like its predecessors, lays such emphasis on the use of the sextant in Coastal Navigation, for which it is invaluable, though still much neglected by yachtsmen despite the advent of plastic sextants, costing less than a hand-bearing compass, but adequate for Coastal work: why it teaches the use of Admiralty Tide Tables for their accuracy and ease of use: and why it includes the Traverse Table.

This edition, like the previous ones, is self-contained in the sense that it can be read understandably and followed throughout without reference to any other book, necessary extracts from tables being provided in the Appendices to enable the worked examples to be followed. The differences from preceding editions, though great, are all by way of up-dating and addition. As regards up-dating, the main new material concerns metric charts and includes my original "1, 2, 3" rule, of acceptably good accuracy, for mental calculation of distance-off from vertical sextant angle observations of metric heights: an original combined fathom/metre lead line design: the introduction of Lowest Astronomical Tide as a datum: and the new buoyage systems, including the IALA system "A" to be introduced into European waters from April 1977 and many examples of which are already established. The additional material consists mainly of two completely new chapters, one dealing with the operation of those radio navigation aids now commonly to be found in yachts, and the other concerned with the practical use, especially for anti-collision navigation, of the simpler Radar installations with which little ships are increasingly being equipped.

And now for the promised practical tip:— The observant will notice that some of the worked exercises in the book, notably some of the tide interpolation examples, now contain distinctly awkward arithmetical calculations instead of merely adhering to interpolation by eye. The latter is, of course, as practical as ever, but the advent of the cheap pocket digital calculator has given the navigator a tool which makes the most awkward arithmetic easy .The inexpensive and simple calculators which have no "memory" are quite adequate but, as sold, they are far from watertight, and semi-conductor integrated circuits, like other "electrics", are allergic to the sea atmosphere in a little ship. Nevertheless, provide yourself with one. Put it in a thin transparent plastic bag, a couple of inches or so longer than the calculator; fold the surplus at the open end of the bag over the back of the calculator; and stick it down with cellotape. You now have a watertight calculator which can stay in its bag until you pull off the tape to take it out of its bag to change the battery, for the keys and figures can be easily seen, and the keys can easily be operated through, the thin plastic material of the sealed bag.

M.J.R.
April, 1977

ACKNOWLEDGMENTS

The grateful thanks of the Author are due to the Hydrographer of the Navy and the Controller of H.M. Stationery Office for permission to take, from official publications, Appendices 1, 2, and 3, Figs. 16 and 17, and those other illustrations individually so indicated; to the Manager for the Owners of *Inman's Nautical Tables*, published by J. D. Potter Ltd. of The Minories, E.C. 3, for permission to take Appendices 4, 5, 6, 7, and 8 from those Tables; and to Messrs. Heath and Company Ltd., Messrs Henry Hughes and Son Ltd., and Messrs. Offshore Instruments Ltd. for permission to illustrate this book with photographs of their instruments.

CONTENTS

LIST OF PLATES

Plate I appears as the Frontispiece of this book, and Plates II to VII are inserted at page 103

CHAPTER I

THE CHART: GENERAL INFORMATION

The task of the little ship navigator falls under two headings, planning and execution. Planning can often be done in the quiet of harbour before a passage starts, and consists in deciding the various courses to be followed over different sections of the passage, how long each section will take, what tides will be experienced, and so on. Execution, which usually has to be done in far less comfortable conditions at sea, consists in carrying out the previously prepared plans, observing and recording the ship's actual progress by whatever means may be available, and if necessary modifying the original plans as circumstances may dictate. The more careful and complete the planning, the easier and safer the execution. Both planning and execution require detailed information about the portion of the earth's surface over which the intended passage lies. The most important source of such information is the Chart, and a study of navigation therefore logically begins with it.

Admiralty Charts. There are many types of chart commercially available, each with its own advantages and disadvantages. Throughout this book, however, it will be presumed, with few and self-evident exceptions, that Admiralty charts are to be used, for these are the standard charts in use by British seamen. Though sometimes a little awkward to stow in very small ships, they are quite practical for such use, and have the paramount advantages of being most complete and precise as to the information given. Moreover, they are easily corrected and kept up to date. Admiralty charts are obtainable from Chart Agents—from whom can also be obtained the Catalogue of Admiralty Charts and Other Publications, in which these charts are listed by number and title. This catalogue contains index

21

charts from which it is possible to see very quickly what is available for any particular area. Section II of the catalogue covers the coasts of the United Kingdom.

Scale. A chart is a map of the sea, *i.e.* a conventionalised picture, on a flat surface, of a portion of the curved surface of the earth. The NATURAL SCALE of a chart is the ratio of the area of the picture to the actual area represented therein. The larger this ratio the smaller the scale and the less the extent of the detail that can be shown. Thus a chart having a natural scale of 1 : 72,000 (corresponding to 1 inch to 1 mile) shows a good deal more detail than one with a natural scale of 1 : 393,000 (corresponding to 1/5th of an inch to 1 mile). *In selecting a chart, therefore, for use in narrow or shallow waters or in an area where it may be necessary to close the land or enter harbour, always choose the largest available scale.*

General Information. The information contained in Admiralty charts is given by means of standardised symbols and abbreviations, which are listed, both for metric and fathom charts, in what is still called Chart 5011 though it is now a booklet. The intending navigator is strongly recommended to familiarise himself with these standard symbols and to carry Chart No. 5011 aboard his ship.

Chart Title. The first thing to look at is the title. This is much more than a mere label and should be read carefully, since it may contain much key information. A typical title is reproduced in Fig. 1. It contains, in addition to a statement of the area charted, such key information as the natural scale, the way in which bearings, soundings, and heights of land, drying banks, or rocks are given, and the datum levels from which such soundings and heights are measured. The surveys on which the chart is based are also included and often further information, such as the exact positions of prominent land features.

Corrections. Admiralty Notices to Mariners. Always see that a chart is up to date, and so far as possible keep it so. Charts as sold by Official Admiralty Chart Agents are corrected up to date at the time of sale, and the corrections incorporated are shown by a string of numbers outside the frame of the chart at the bottom. *Always look at these numbers when acquiring a chart.* They represent the years and numbers of the ADMIRALTY NOTICES TO MARINERS, which are issued regularly.

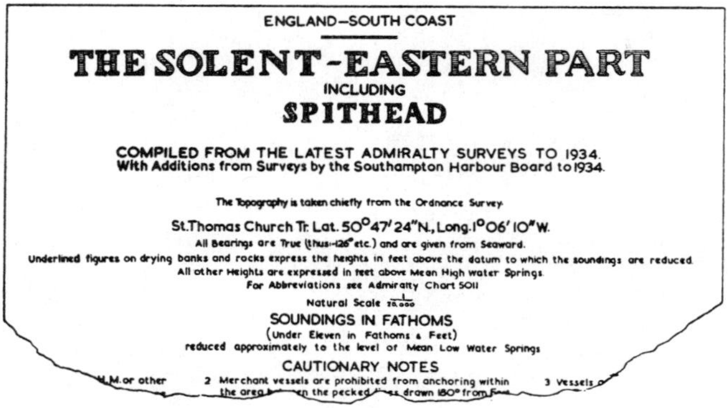

FIG. 1.

(*From an old British Admiralty Fathom Chart.*)

These notices, which are numbered in sequence, are careful, plain-language statements of changes of interest to seamen. They deal with such matters as changes in the position or details of buoys or lightships, changes in harbour lights, positions or removal of wrecks, and so on. Agents will supply Notices to Mariners, as they are issued, for a small subscription, and the little ship master should make a practice of taking them and incorporating in waterproof ink those which affect him. *When incorporating a correction always add the number of the Notice to the list of corrections at the bottom of the chart,* so that it is always possible to see which was the last correction made. Corrections from *temporary or preliminary notices* should be inserted in *pencil* so that they can be rubbed out if cancelled later.

True Compass Roses.   Circular Notation.   Several compass roses are usually provided.   Each rose always includes an outer circle or TRUE COMPASS ROSE which is divided in degrees

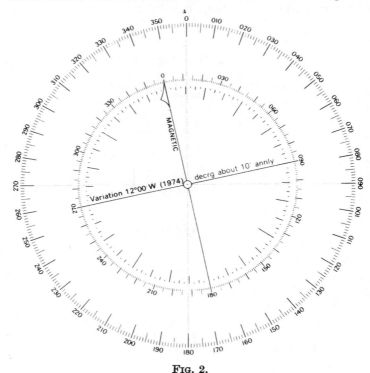

FIG. 2.

(From a British Admiralty Metric Chart.)

from 0° at the true N, clockwise through E, S, and W to 359°. These true roses are so oriented that a line between 0° and 180° is true N and S.   The outer ring of Fig. 2 is a true compass rose. The true direction between two positions on a chart may therefore be obtained as shown in Fig. 3, by placing the edge of a parallel ruler across these positions (Nab Tower and No

Mans Land Fort), and then running it across the chart until
the edge passes through the middle of a rose. The required
direction is then read off where the edge cuts the circle. True
courses or directions are always written in so-called CIRCULAR

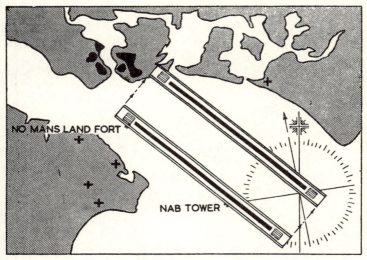

FIG. 3.

NOTATION, thus: 175° 253° 18°. To avoid errors it is recommended always to speak of them in three figures, thus:
one-seven-five, for a hundred and seventy-five degrees, *two-
five-three* for two hundred and fifty-three degrees, and *owe-one-
eight* for eighteen degrees.

Magnetic Compass Roses. Quadrantal Notation. On some
general charts only true compass roses are provided, but in
most cases MAGNETIC COMPASS ROSES are also given. These,
when provided, are concentrically within the true compass
roses and are oriented so that the N point corresponds to
magnetic instead of true N. The middle ring of Fig. 2 is a
magnetic compass rose. In modern charts, degree markings are
given in the same way as on a true rose but there are older charts

about in which they are numbered 1 to 90 clockwise between N and E and between S and W, and 1 to 90 anti-clockwise between S and E and between N and W. This is called QUADRANTAL NOTATION, and a magnetic course or direction is given by stating the number of degrees E or W of N or S with N or S first and E or W last. Thus a magnetic direction half-way between N and E is written N 45° E, and one a third of the way between S and E is written S 30° E. New Admiralty charts are produced with the magnetic compass rose, like the true rose, divided into degrees numbered consecutively clockwise up to 359°, and quadrantal notation may gradually disappear. In addition a magnetic compass rose in POINTS NOTATION (this will be described later) is usually provided.

Magnetic Variation. A magnetic rose is " twisted " in relation to a true rose, for the N point of the former is magnetic north, whereas that of the latter is true N. The angle between magnetic N and true N is called the VARIATION. It is not constant, but varies all over the surface of the earth. It also changes slowly with time. Therefore, if using a magnetic rose to lay off a course or bearing *always use the one nearest to your position on the chart. Also make sure it is still correct at the date you are using it.* This can be ascertained from the information printed across the E–W line of the rose. In Fig. 2. this information is given as "Variation 12° 00′ W (1974) decrg about 10′ annly". There are 360 degrees (°) in the circle and 60 minutes (′) in one degree. Since the N of the magnetic rose, in this case, points to W of that of the true rose, the variation is westerly. Suppose you were using this magnetic rose twelve years after 1974. The variation will have decreased by $12 \times 10′ = 120′ = 2°$ so the rose as printed will by then be 2° wrong. *It is recommended, however, not to use the magnetic roses at all for laying off courses, etc., but always to use the true roses, applying the variation by simple addition or subtraction in the manner which will be described later in the chapters on the compass.*

Isogonic Lines. On charts without magnetic roses, and sometimes on charts with them, information about variation is given by means of ISOGONIC LINES, or magnetic meridians, as they are often called. These are lines drawn across the chart joining positions on the earth's surface where the variation is the same. The required information about variation—its value in a stated year and its annual rate of increase or decrease—is printed on each line. On small-area charts these lines appear straight, though they are actually parts of irregularly curved lines going all over the globe. *Note that the direction of an isogonic line does not matter to you: only its position and the information printed on it.* To find the variation at any place on such a chart, look for the nearest isogonic line and use the information printed on it.

Point Roses. On charts with magnetic roses there is printed inside the degree markings of the magnetic rose a ring consisting of 128 unnumbered marks. These are POINT markings. The point notation will be described later in the chapters on the compass: it is sufficient here to say that there are 32 points in the circle, so each point is $11\frac{1}{4}°$ (360 divided by 32), and the 128 marks are therefore quarter points. *Again it is recommended not to use the point roses for chart work, but always the true roses.* If, however, it is desired to convert a course or bearing which is already worked out from points to Magnetic or vice versa—for example, if the ship's compass is marked in points and quarter points—it is convenient to use the point rose and the magnetic rose for the conversion. Since these roses are concentric, similarly oriented, and close together, it is easy to read off from one on to the other with the aid of a straight edge.

Soundings. In fathom charts, now being gradually superceded by metric charts, soundings i.e. depths of water below chart datum, are usually given in fathoms (1 fm. = 6 ft.) in the form of numbers printed in the positions in question. Soundings in less than 11 fathoms are commonly given in fathoms and feet thus, 8_4 for 8 fms. 4 ft., or fathoms and fractions thus, $8\frac{1}{2}$. On some charts, notably the very large-scale charts known as harbour plans, soundings may be in feet, while on foreign charts they may be in other units again, *e.g.* metres. The introduction of Admiralty charts with soundings in metres and decimetres commenced in 1970 and is still proceeding. On these charts depths below datum are usually given in metres and decimetres if below 20 metres and in metres elsewhere. *Blank spaces without soundings (there are few such spaces in home water charts) mean that no soundings have been taken there.*

Drying Banks and Rocks. In fathom charts the height to which banks and rocks dry out at low water is normally given in feet by means of underlined figures in the appropriate positions. Thus *4* on a sandbank means that, at low water springs, that position is 4 ft. above the datum of the chart. The corresponding information is also given by underlined figures in metric charts but the figures are metres and decimetres.

Chart Datum. Obviously the depth of water at any place varies with the tide, and accordingly the soundings given on a chart are depths below an arbitrarily chosen level. This is the DATUM of the chart. By international agreement the various Hydrographic Authorities of the world adopt datums corresponding to some " plane so low that the tide will but seldom fall below it." On many older Admiralty charts the datum is still the level of Mean Low Water Spring Tides (M.L.W.S.) but it has been decided to adopt a somewhat lower level—that of Lowest Astronomical Tide (L.A.T.)—as the standard chart datum. This level is that of the lowest low water reached in normal meteorological conditions. Admiralty charts, with soundings corrected to this level, are being issued, but it will be some time before uniformity is reached in this respect. The same datum that is used for soundings is also used for heights of drying banks and rocks. *In all cases the datum is given in the title.* Note that the depths on a chart with **M.L.W.S. as datum** *are not the least depths which can possibly occur,* though they are usually nearly so.

Land Heights. Datum for Heights. Land heights are normally given in feet or metres above a datum which corresponds to approximately the *highest* sea-level ordinarily encountered. In charts based on British surveys this datum is usually the level of Mean High Water Spring tides (M.H.W.S.). Figures **bracketed** against islands or rocks which are always above water indicate heights above this datum.

Tidal Information. Most charts give a good deal of information about tides (up and down movements of the sea), either in tabular form or in the positions concerned, or both. The information given is not always the same but often includes High Water Full and Change (H.W.F. & C.), Low Water Full and Change (L.W.F. & C.), height (above datum) of Mean High Water (H.W.) springs, height (above datum) of Mean H.W. neaps, and Mean Level at various places. These terms will be explained later in the chapter dealing with tides. It is sufficient here to say that H.W.F. & C. is the time of H.W. on days of full or new moon, and L.W.F. & C. is the time of L.W. on such days. The time is given in hours and minutes, the hours being in Roman numerals and the minutes in ordinary numerals. Fig. 4

Tidal Information

| Place | Lunitidal Intervals | | Height above datum of soundings | | | Datum to which Soundings are reduced |
	H.W.F. & C.	L.W.F. & C.	Mean H.W. Springs	Mean L.W. Neaps	Mean Level	
Portsmouth	XIh 30m	XVIh 46m	13 feet	10 feet	7 feet	6ft. 4ins. on Stone Tide Gauge No.VI Portsmouth Dockyard or 8·17ft. Datum (Liverpool).
Ryde	XIh 20m		13½ "	10 "		27·9ft. below a 2? Dover and Co brass pl of th
Cowes	XIh 36m	XVIh 46m	11 "	8½ "	5½ "	
Southampton	Xh 55m	XVIh 29m	13½ "			
	XIIh 57m					
Calshot Castle	X?					

Fig. 4.

(From an old British Admiralty Fathom Chart.)

is part of a table of tidal information from the old fathom chart for the Eastern Part of the Solent.

Tidal Stream Information. Much information is usually given about tidal streams (horizontal movements of the sea) either in the form of arrows or in tabular form or both. The arrow form is now adopted on charts only when the available information is incomplete. The tables usually give the directions, in degrees true, and rates in knots, for both spring and neap tides, of the tidal streams which occur in various positions on the chart. These positions are stated in latitude and longitude and identified by letters or numbers which are printed on the chart in these positions. Fig. 5 is part of a table of tidal stream information from the old chart for the Eastern Part of the Solent. *These tidal stream tables are the most important and useful source of tidal stream information available to the navigator and should always be used for the actual navigation.* If you are about to make a passage on a particular day, look at the appropriate chart to find any of these lettered or numbered positions on or

Tidal Streams

	Hours	Position ⊕ Lat.50°43′7N.Long 1°03′9W			⊕ Horse & Dean Sand Lat.50°45′9N.Long 1°04′1W			⊕ Spithead Lat.50°45′1N Long 1°06′2W			⊕ off the Ridge Lat.50°46′2″1.Long 1°05′2W		
		Direction	Rate Sp	Np	Direction	Rate Sp	Np	Direction	Rate Sp	Np		Direction	Rate Sp Np
0330	6				77°	0·4kn	0·2kn	90°	0·7kn	0·4kn	6	44°	0·2kn 0·2
0430	5	14P	15kn	0·8kn	90°	1·2 ·	0·6 ·	109°	1·1 ·	0·5 ·	5	67°	0·2 · 0·2 ·
0530	4	14P	15 ·	0·6 ·	85°	0·8 ·	0·6 ·	117°	1·3 ·	0·6 ·	4	34°	0·2
0630	3	130°	08·	0·4 ·	47°	0·2 ·	0·1 ·	115°	0·8 ·	0·4 ·	4	342°	0·2
0730	2	Turning			285°	0·5·	0·3 ·	67°	0·3 ·	0·1 ·	4	334°	0·2
0830	1	310°	08·	0·4 ·	278°	1·0 ·	0·5 ·	320°	0·5 ·	0·3 ·		317°	
0930	H.W.	310°	1·1 ·	0·6 ·	275°	1·1 ·	0·5 ·	302°	1·2 ·	0·6 ·	H.W.	314°	
1030	1	310°	1·3 ·	0·7 ·	270°	0·7·	0·3 ·	295°	1·6 ·	0·8 ·	1	286°	
1130	2	310°	0·7 ·	0·4 ·	227°	0·2 ·	0·1 ·	289°	1·4 ·	0·7 ·	2	239°	
1230	3	152°	1·0 ·	0·5 ·	121°	0·5 ·	0·3 ·	255°	0·6 ·	0·3 ·	3	146°	
1330	4	152°	1·0 ·	0·5 ·	112°	0·6 ·	0·3 ·	158°	0·4 ·	0·2 ·	3	142°	
1430	5	141°	1·3 ·	0·7 ·	Turning			124°	0·4 ·	0·2 ·	5	143°	
1530	6	141°	1·3 ·	0·7 ·	69°	0·2 ·	0·1 ·	85°	0·6 ·	0·3 ·	6	175°	

FIG. 5.

(From an old British Admiralty Fathom Chart.)

near your intended track, and mark them lightly in pencil by a large ring or arrow so that you can find them again quickly when at sea, possibly in a badly lit cabin at night. Also, as indicated in Fig. 5, strike out in pencil all those columns in the table which relate to positions too far away from your intended track to interest you. Then look up, for the day in question, the time of H.W. at the standard or reference port (Portsmouth in Fig. 5) and insert that time in pencil alongside the H.W. line in the table. Also insert the appropriate times alongside the other lines for the different hours before and after H.W. If you are keeping Summer Time aboard, insert the times in Summer Time (the tide tables give H.W., etc., for places in the United Kingdom in G.M.T.). Thus, if the time of H.W. Portsmouth is 08.30 (G.M.T.) and you are keeping British Summer Time, write 09.30 opposite H.W., 08.30 opposite 1 hour before, 07.30 opposite 2 hours before . . . and so on as indicated outside the frame of the table in Fig. 5. This simple preparation will save much trouble at sea, for you have only to look at the ship's clock and the appropriate uncancelled part of the table to see the tidal stream at a glance at any time.

Sea-Bottom Information. Fathom Lines. Much useful information about the sea bottom is given either in words, *e.g.* " Foul Ground," or in the form of standardised letters or abbreviations which will be found dotted about the chart, and which are listed in Chart No. 5011, *e.g.* " Ck " for chalk. In addition sea-bottom contours are given on fathom charts with different sorts of lines for different depths; thus a chain line of dashes and double dots is a 20 fm. line, one with dashes and single dots is a 10 fm. line, a line of groups of four dots means 4 fm., and so on. On metric charts sea bottom contours are given by simple thin lines with gaps in which the appropriate depths, in metres, are printed.

Symbols. Abbreviations. Many of the symbols used are self-evident, being in fact conventionalised pictures of the things they represent. Thus, for example, light vessels, buoys, above-water wrecks, cliffy coastlines, and sandbanks, all look more or less like these things. Others, though not pictures of the things they represent, directly suggest them—*e.g.* different sorts of anchors for anchorages for different sizes of ships, and crosses (on shore) for churches. It has been said that the use of crosses (at sea) for rocks is also of this type by suggesting tombstones! In the cases of light vessels, buoys, and beacons whose symbols occupy a fair amount of space, the actual position is the centre of the base and is usually indicated by a small circle. Thus, in Fig. 6 which represents a light vessel, the position is the centre of the small circle X. Information about navigation aiding lights, and so on, is given by means of standardised abbreviations (see Chart 5011), and, in general, the amount of information given is increased as the scale of the chart increases.

FIG. 6.

Colours in Admiralty Charts. On the majority of fairly recent Admiralty fathom charts shallow water areas are emphasised by a blue tint. In most cases areas between the H.W. line and the 3 fm line are coloured blue and a narrow ribbon of blue is added on the shallow side of the 6 fm line. On metric charts areas between the H.W. line and the 5 metre line are coloured blue and a narrow ribbon of blue is added on the shallow side of the 10 metre line: areas which dry out are tinted a pale green: and land areas are tinted yellow.

Admiralty charts present a vast amount of information in a form which lends itself to quick appreciation by those who have made themselves familiar with the conventions. *Therefore, if when using a chart you find some item which is strange to you, look it up straightaway in Chart No. 5011.*

CHAPTER II

THE CHART: GENERAL USE AND CONSTRUCTION

Latitude and Longitude. Since in the open sea there are usually no recognisable objects in known fixed positions, it is necessary, in order to define a position, to have some frame of reference. For this purpose two imaginary lines at right angles to one another on the surface of the earth are adopted. The first is the EQUATOR, a line drawn round the earth half-way between the North and South Poles. The second is the

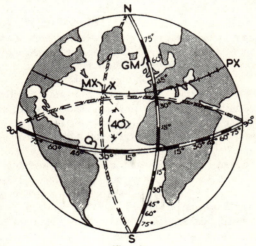

FIG. 7.

MERIDIAN OF GREENWICH, a line drawn from Pole to Pole and passing through Greenwich.

In Fig. 7 N and S are the North and South Poles respectively, Q is the equator, and GM is Greenwich Meridian; and it will

33

be obvious that the position of any place such as X can be
defined by stating how much it is N or S of the Equator and
how much it is E or W of Greenwich Meridian.   The former is
the LATITUDE of the place and the latter the LONGITUDE.
Latitude and longitude are measured in angles at the earth's
centre and at the Poles respectively.   Since the earth approxi-
mates closely to a sphere and may, for present purposes, be so
regarded, to go from the Equator to either Pole along Greenwich meridian is to go through a quarter of a circle, *i.e.* 90°,
and to go right round the earth along the equator is to go
through a complete circle, *i.e.* 360°.   The latitude of any
place may therefore be defined by stating the angle (not more
than 90°) it is N or S of the Equator, and its longitude may be
defined by stating the angle (not more than 180°) it is E or W
of Greenwich Meridian.   Thus the position X in Fig. 7 is
40° N 30° W.

Parallels and Meridians.   A circular line drawn round the
earth parallel to the Equator is termed a PARALLEL OF
LATITUDE, and clearly all places on the same parallel have the
same latitude.   In Fig. 7, PX is the parallel through X, *i.e.*
40° N parallel.   Similarly any line drawn, like Greenwich
Meridian, from Pole to Pole at right angles to the Equator, is
termed a MERIDIAN and all places on the same meridian have
the same longitude.   In Fig. 7, MX is the meridian of X, *i.e.*
30° W.   Note that meridians are all semi-circles of the same size,
whereas parallels get smaller and smaller as they approach
the Poles.   The same angle measured along any meridian is,
therefore, always the same distance on the earth's surface,
but this is not the case with the parallels, a given angle
measured along the Equator covering a longer distance than
the same angle measured along a parallel nearer a Pole.

Nautical Mile.   Cable.   Knot.   Since a given angle measured
along a meridian is always the same distance, it is convenient
to employ this form of measurement for the unit of distance.
The unit adopted for navigational purposes is the NAUTICAL
or SEA MILE, which is the distance measured along a meridian
of 1 minute (1′) of latitude.   Thus, if one place has a latitude
of 52° 17′ N and another place, of the same longitude, has

a latitude of 52° 18', the second place is 1 sea mile N of the first. Since in fact the earth is not exactly a perfect sphere, but flattens a little towards the Poles, the length on the earth's surface of 1' of latitude is not in fact exactly the same every-where, but to avoid difficulties from this cause, a mean value of 6080 ft. is adopted for the sea mile. It may be noted that this is appreciably longer than the English statute mile (the land mile) which is only 5280 ft., so that 13 sea miles=(very nearly) 15 land miles. The sea mile is sub-divided into 10 CABLES, so that 1 cable=(very nearly) 200 yards.

The unit of speed at sea is the KNOT, which is 1 sea mile per hour. It is worth remembering, for purposes of quick mental arithmetic, that 1 knot=(very nearly) 100 ft. per minute.

Mercator's Projection. Since the earth's surface is curved and a chart is flat, it is necessary to adopt some form of projection to enable the latter to represent a portion of the former, and it will be apparent that whatever form of pro-jection is used, some distortion will be introduced. The only form of projection which will be dealt with in this book is MERCATOR'S PROJECTION, for all charts—other than certain large-area oceanic charts, polar charts, and a few other special purpose charts—are either in this projection or (in the case of harbour plans and other small area charts) are on a projection (gnomonic) which for practical navigation by such charts, may be treated by the little ship navigator as though it were Mercator. It is most unlikely that the master of the little ship will encounter anything else in coastal navigation. It is important to under-stand the nature of the distortion present in a Mercator chart. First there is an E–W " stretching " distortion, which is greater the further from the Equator, and which is such that the meridians, which in fact are circular lines converging on the Poles, appear as parallel straight lines at right angles to the Equator. Secondly, there is a N–S " stretching " distortion, which also becomes greater the further from the Equator, and is such that, despite the E–W " stretching," the degrees of latitude everywhere bear the same proportion to the degrees of longitude that they do on earth. This will be better understood by considering an imaginary chart-manufacturing process.

Suppose Fig. 8 is a model globe coated with thin rubber and

correctly drawn out with the various land areas to scale, and suppose also it is required to make a Mercator chart of the area ABCD bounded by two meridians and the Equator and a parallel north of it. We begin by marking out the edge parallels and meridians with scales of latitude and longitude

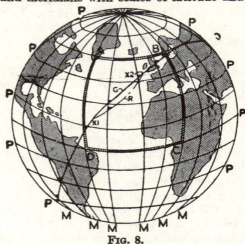

FIG. 8.

so that the area is framed with these scales. We then cut round the model globe along the Equator and along the parallel corresponding to the top edge of the area, and remove the spherically curved ring of rubber we have thus freed. We now cut through the ring along the meridians at the side edges AD, BC of the area to obtain Fig. 9. We now stretch

the rubber sideways, applying, however, no stretch at the Equator edge, CD, but merely flattening this edge down (an action which brings the corners C, D further apart), but increasing the stretch northwards of the Equator until the meridians become parallel straight lines. At the same time we apply stretch upwards in proportion everywhere

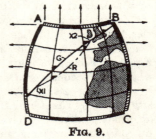

FIG. 9.

to the sideways stretch, so that the more we had to pull sideways in any latitude to make the meridians into parallel straight lines, the more we pull upwards to separate the parallels in that latitude. The result is as shown in Fig. 10. The rubber is

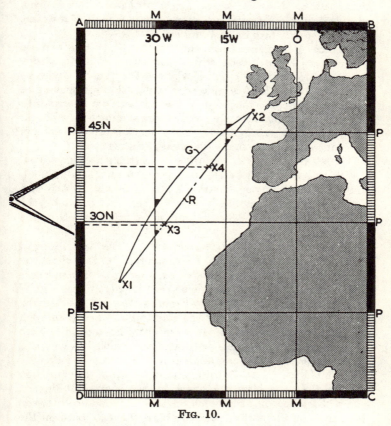

Fig. 10.

now flat, and the meridians M have become parallel straight lines at right angles to the parallels P, which are also parallel straight lines. We have now made our Mercator chart. Note what has happened to the edge scales. The two longitude scales, top and bottom of the chart, are now alike, *though a minute along them still does not represent a mile except on the Equator.* The two latitude scales along the sides of the chart are also alike, and a minute along them still represents a mile, *but the minute divisions are no longer of the same length from top to bottom of the chart. In other words, the scale of the chart is not constant, but varies with latitude.*

Distance Measurement on the Chart. Since the minute divisions of the longitude scales (the top and bottom edge scales) do not represent miles, whereas the minute divisions of the latitude scales (the side edge scales) do represent miles correctly, *but only in their own latitudes,* there are two rules to remember in using the scales to measure distance on a chart:

1. NEVER USE THE LONGITUDE SCALES (the top and bottom edge scales) FOR DISTANCE MEASUREMENT.
2. ALWAYS USE THE LATITUDE SCALES (the side edge scales) IN THE LATITUDE OF THE DISTANCE TO BE MEASURED.

Thus, in measuring the distance X_3 to X_4 in Fig. 10, the part of the scale which should be used is that indicated by the dividers, and *if this is done* the number of minutes will be the distance in miles.

Latitude and Longitude Measurement. The latitude and longitude of any place can be measured on the chart by directly using the appropriate edge scales. To measure latitude, orient the parallel rule so that its edge lies E and W through the place and read off where the edge cuts a side scale. To measure longitude, orient the rule to lie N and S through the place and note where the edge cuts the top or bottom scale. One of the parallels and meridians which will be found drawn across the chart can be used for orienting the rule.

Rhumb Lines. Great Circles. A minor effect of the distortion introduced into a Mercator chart is that a straight line on such a chart does not represent the shortest distance between two points on the earth's surface unless they are both on the same meridian. Obviously the shortest distance between two such points is along a circle which exactly bisects the earth. Such a circle is shown at G in Figs. 8 and 9 and is termed a GREAT CIRCLE. It will be observed that it does not cut the meridians at the same angle and therefore, to follow it say from X_1 to X_2, means altering course all the time—an obvious inconvenience. There is, however, a track R (see Figs. 8 and 9) from X_1 to X_2 which is only slightly longer than along G (not sufficiently longer to matter on any but very long transoceanic passages), which cuts all the meridians at the same angle and can, therefore, be followed by a constant course. Such a track is termed a RHUMB LINE. The effect of the distortion of the chart is, as shown in Fig. 10, to transform R into a straight line, so that when a straight line constant course is laid off on the chart and followed, what is actually followed is a rhumb line.

It may be noted, before closing this chapter, that Mercator's projection is not used for polar charts, because near the Poles the distortion becomes so great as to render the system impracticable. Moreover, areas nearer the Poles appear " larger than life " as compared with areas nearer the Equator. This is of no navigational importance in practice (*though it emphasises the importance of using the proper parts of the latitude scale for distance measurement*), but it accounts for such facts as that Sweden looks a good deal larger than Spain in a Mercator projection of Europe, though in fact it is a good deal smaller.

CHAPTER III

TIDES

A tide is an up-and-down or vertical movement of water affecting depth below the sea surface. The term is often loosely used also to mean a horizontal movement or flow of the sea. Strictly speaking, however, this is a " tidal stream," and while, no doubt, seamen will continue to speak of " cheating a tide " or " stemming a tide," instead of " cheating a tidal *stream*," such terminology is really inaccurate, though convenient. Whatever the terms used it is important to distinguish mentally between a tide and a tidal stream.

General Theory. The full theory of tides is far too complex for inclusion here, nor is it at all necessary to the master of the little ship. An appreciation of the broad principles involved, however, is helpful.

Tides are a manifestation of the law of gravity and are due to the joint gravity attractions of the sun and moon. The moon revolves round the earth, making one revolution in approximately 30 days, and the earth revolves round the sun in approximately 365 days. Therefore every 30 days, approximately, the moon comes between the sun and the earth, and approximately 15 days later the three bodies again come into the same straight line, this time with the sun on one side of the earth and the moon on the other. Since the moon shines by the reflected light of the sun, it shows us a darkened face when it is between us and the sun. The sun and moon are then said to be in conjunction and it is new moon. When the sun and moon are on opposite sides of us they are said to be in opposition; the moon is fully lit on the side towards us and it is full moon.

Fig. 11 is a diagram of the conjunction or new moon condition. In Fig. 11 the earth, E, is represented as covered all over by a " skin " of water, the thickness of the skin being much exaggerated in the figure. Both the sun and moon subject the earth, including, of course, the water on its surface, to the force of gravitational attraction. This is a natural force of attraction which occurs between any two bodies which

Fig. 11.

are spaced apart, and is directly proportional to their mass and inversely proportional to the square of the distance between them. In other words, the bigger the bodies, the more is the attracting force between them; the further apart the bodies, the less is the attracting force between them, the force decreasing with increase of separation much more rapidly than it increases with increase of mass. Consider first the effect of the moon alone. The earth being a solid body the force of the moon may be regarded as exerted on the earth's centre. This, however, is not so near the moon as the water immediately on one side. Similarly the water on the opposite side of the earth is still further away from the moon than is the earth's centre. Accordingly the moon exerts most force on the water nearest it, rather less force on the solid earth, and still less force on the water furthest away. The result is, therefore, to pile up the water after the fashion indicated in Fig. 11 giving high waters at H.W.1 and H.W.2 and low waters at positions L.W.1 and L.W.2. half-way between them. The moon's tidal effect is thus due to the different gravitational forces exerted by the moon at H.W.1, E, and H.W.2. The sun's tidal effect differs only in degree. Although the sun is further away from us than the moon, it is so enormously bigger that its total gravitational pull is greater; nevertheless its tidal effect is smaller. This is because its distance is so large that the gravitational forces exerted by it at H.W.1 and H.W.2 are more nearly the same than in the case of the moon. Actually the ratio of moon's tidal effect to sun's tidal effect is about 7 to 3. With the bodies in the relative positions of Fig. 11, the sun's tidal effect is added to the moon's, producing *high* high waters at H.W.1 and H.W.2, and *low* low waters at L.W.1 and L.W.2—in other words SPRING TIDES. Practically the

FIG. 12.

same effect is produced in the full moon, or opposition, condition shown in Fig. 12, for here again the sun and moon are in the same straight line and their tidal effects reinforce one another. When the sun and moon are not in line, each tries to produce its own high water underneath itself, and the result is the production of a sort of compromise high water with the moon the dominant partner. The condition at the first and last quarters, *i.e.* half-way between those of Figs. 11 and 12, is illustrated in Fig. 13, which shows one of the two " quad-

FIG. 13.

rature " positions, as they are called. In this case the sun and moon tidal effects are at right angles to one another and therefore do not reinforce one another. The moon, as the dominant partner, still produces a high water, but it is the lowest high water—in other words NEAP TIDES. To summarise, therefore, at new and full moon there are spring tides with the greatest variation of depth of water—highest high water and lowest low water. Half-way between these times, at the two quarters, there are neap tides with the least variation of depth of water—lowest high water and highest low water.

High Water Full and Change of Moon. As the earth rotates, the positions at which the high waters occur travel round it, so that there is a travelling wave of tide. Note that this is a true wave. The water only moves up and down and not horizontally as the wave passes. The action is like that of a ruler placed under a table cloth so as to lift it a little and then drawn along. As the ruler passes, the cloth comes up in a wave and then goes down again; the cloth does not move horizontally. The speed of the wave, where unobstructed, is more than 1000 miles per hour and its height from crest to trough is about four or five feet in mid-Atlantic. When, however, the wave is obstructed by shallow or constricted water—as in the English Channel—it is slowed down, especially at the sides where friction is greatest. Because it is slowed down it piles up and increases its height. Thus, as the tide wave comes up the narrowing English Channel it increases in height until, on the French coast near the Channel Islands, it reaches 35 to 40 ft. or so. Also, since the slowing effect is most at the sides of a channel, the wave in mid-Channel reaches somewhere between Dover and Boulogne when the northern edge is only in the neighbourhood of Selsey Bill. The time of arrival of the tide wave at any particular place accordingly depends upon topography, and since topographical conditions are practically constant we should expect, from theory, that the time of H.W. at any place for a given condition of sun and moon would always be the same. This is borne out in practice, and on many charts the time of high water at various places on days of full and new moon is given. As will be obvious from Figs. 11 and 12, a full moon crosses the meridian at midnight and a new moon at mid-day. If, therefore, the obstruction encountered by the tide wave is such that it reaches some particular port 4 hours (say) after the full or new moon's transit of the meridian, the time of the next H.W. at that port on those days will be 4 a.m. (0400) and 4 p.m. (1600 hrs.) respectively. This statement of the time of H.W. at a port in terms of the lag after full or new (*i.e.* change of) moon is called HIGH WATER FULL AND CHANGE (H.W.F. & C.). H.W.F. & C. Dover is $XI^h 24^m$, so the next H.W. at Dover after a full moon (midnight) is 11.24 and the next H.W. after a new moon (mid-day) is 23.24. Low WATER FULL AND CHANGE (L.W.F. & C.), which is often given as well, indicates, in similar fashion, the times of L.W. after a full or new moon.

High Water between Full and New Moon. Since the lunar day is approximately 24 hours 50 minutes, the time of H.W. at any place is approximately 50 minutes later each day. It is therefore possible to calculate the time of H.W. approximately for any place whose H.W.F. & C. is given, by allowing 50 minutes a day from the nearest full or new moon. If the nearest full or new moon is past, add the appropriate number of 50-minute intervals to H.W.F. & C.; if the nearest full or new moon is ahead, subtract them. In the absence of any better information the interval between successive high and low waters may be assumed to be 6 hours 13 minutes and the interval between successive high waters 12 hours 25 minutes.

Example. Required the times of H.W. at Dover on 9th December, 1976.

Full Moon 6th December.	
H.W.F. & C.	1124
Add 3 days at 50 mins per day	230
(Second) H.W. 9 December	1354
Subtract 12^h 25^m for First H.W.	1225
(First) H.W. 9th December	0129
High Waters at 0129 and 1354	

The results obtained by this method are very approximate and errors of an hour or so can often occur. It should therefore not be employed except where approximate results are good enough. *For navigational purposes tide tables should always be used.*

Rise and Fall of Tide. Mean Tide Level. Between H.W. and L.W. the tide rises or falls approximately harmonically after the manner of a piston in a cylinder when the crankshaft is rotated at constant speed. Fig. 14 is a pictorial representation

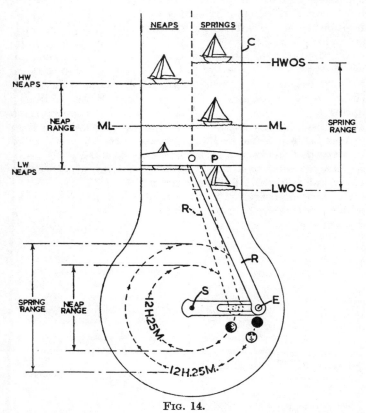

Fig. 14.

of this mechanical analogy. In this figure the piston P moves up and down in the cylinder C under the action of the connecting rod R driven by the crankshaft S rotating at constant speed (one revolution in 12 hours 25 minutes), and the level of the surface of the water on the piston accordingly moves up and down. The *speed* of the up and down movement is at a maximum in the middle of the piston travel, and falls away to nothing at top and bottom of the travel. The *amount* of the travel depends on the throw of the crank. In Fig. 14 this is illustrated as variable by sliding the big-end E between the positions shown in full and dotted lines. The result produced is analogous to the varying effect of the moon during its change from new or full to quadrature. The full-line position, which corresponds to new or full moon, causes the water-level to vary between the lines marked H.W.O.S. and L.W.O.S. (High Water Ordinary Springs and Low Water Ordinary Springs). The dotted line position (which corresponds to first or last quarter) causes the level to vary between the lines marked H.W. neaps and L.W. neaps. *In all positions of adjustment of the throw of the crank, i.e. for all states of the moon, the level oscillates about the same mean position*, which is that of the line marked M.L. (MEAN LEVEL).

Height and Range. The HEIGHT of a tide at any time is, simply, the height of the water surface at that time above chart datum, and the RANGE of a tide is the amount by which

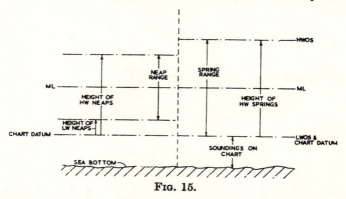

Fig. 15.

the water surface ranges up or down between H.W. and L.W., *i.e.* the height of H.W. *minus* the height of L.W. These terms are illustrated in Fig. 15 and, as respects range, in Fig. 14

also, where SPRING RANGE and NEAP RANGE are indicated. Since the height of the tide at any time is the height of the water surface *above* chart datum and the soundings given on the chart are the depths of the sea bottom *below* chart datum, the depth of water at any place as taken by the lead is equal to the sounding as given by the chart, plus the height of the tide at the time. In some places the sea surface occasionally falls below the chart datum (H.W.O.S.) used on the older charts and, on such occasions a cast of the lead gives a reading equal to the sounding on that chart *minus* the height.

Reduction to Soundings. Duration. Interval. It is often required to correlate a cast of the lead with the soundings given on the chart. Thus, when approaching Chichester from the S, the soundings on the chart reduce from about 8 or 9 fathoms some three miles off the bar to about 1 fathom near the bar. In thickish weather it would be useful to take a cast of the lead, subtract the height of the tide from it, and thus obtain the corresponding chart sounding to help ascertain the position. This conversion of an actual cast into a chart sounding is called REDUCTION TO SOUNDINGS, and is an important part of navigation. To make it we must know the height of L.W., the height of H.W., the DURATION of the tide (how long it takes to go from H.W. to L.W. or vice-versa) and the INTERVAL (how long we are, at the time, from L.W.).

Rough-and-Ready Calculations. A quick, rough-and-ready working which will give a fair approximation in most cases, may be made by assuming a duration of 6 hours for a tide and assuming that its rise or fall is such that the height changes $\frac{1}{16}$ in the first and last hours, $\frac{1}{4}$ in the first and last two hours, and $\frac{1}{2}$ in the first and last three hours—easily remembered figures in simple square root relationship: $\frac{1}{16}$, $\frac{1}{4}$, $\frac{1}{2}$. Thus a rising tide is assumed to rise by $\frac{1}{16}$ of its range by the end of the first hour; $\frac{1}{4}$ by the end of the second; $\frac{1}{2}$ by the end of the third; $\frac{3}{4}$ by the end of the fourth; and $\frac{15}{16}$ by the end of the fifth. If springs H.W. height only is known, neaps H.W. height may be assumed to be $\frac{3}{4}$ of it and L.W. springs may be taken as zero. H.W. height on days between springs and neaps may be estimated by rough interpolation, remembering it takes approximately seven days to go from springs to neaps. Thus, if it is three or four days after a full or new moon, assume the height to be half-way between spring and neap heights.

> *Example.* At about 1800 G.M.T., approaching Shoreham on a day four days after New Moon, a cast of the lead gives 4 fms. 2 ft. H.W. Springs Shoreham about 20 ft. H.W. at about 1500. Reduce to soundings.
>
> H.W. Springs=20 ft. L.W. Springs=0 ft. ∴ Mean Level (M.L.)= 10 ft.
>
> H.W. Neaps=20 × $\frac{3}{4}$=15 ft.
>
> Since it is 4 days after a new moon, H.W. height may be taken as about 17 ft. which is 7 ft. above M.L. and L.W. height as 3 ft. (7 ft. below M.L.).
>
> Range for the day=17—3=14 ft.
>
> 1800=3 hours after H.W.=half tide. Half range=7 ft.
>
> ∴ height at time of cast=17—7=10 ft.=1 fm. 4 ft.
>
> ∴ reduction to sounding=4 fm. 2 ft.—1 fm. 4 ft.=2 fm. 4 ft. on chart.

It is emphasised that this sort of calculation, though better than nothing, is very rough and ready and makes several assumptions which are likely to be wrong, *e.g.*:—the assumptions that tides rise or fall in 6 hours, that spring L.W. heights are zero, that the change from springs to neaps is proportional with time, and so on. Therefore, although the method may be used to give fairly approximate answers if nothing better is available, *make a practice of using the Admiralty Tide Tables*, which will give answers much more accurately, and, once you are used to them, much more quickly.

CHAPTER IV

ADMIRALTY TIDE TABLES

Admiralty Tide Tables are issued annually, Volume I covering British and European Waters and including the Mediterranean. They are extremely full and complete, enable accurate results to be obtained and are quick and easy to use. Moreover they are so compiled that it is possible to see at a glance when a "short cut" in working out a tide may be taken without introducing appreciable error. Their habitual use cannot be too strongly recommended.

Standard Ports. The tide tables divide ports into two classes, STANDARD and SECONDARY ports. The former are contained in Part I of the volume and are alphabetically indexed inside the front cover. This part of the tables gives the times and heights in metres and feet of H.W. and L.W., day by day, for each port throughout the year, with the latitudes and longitudes of the places for which the tides are predicted. The predictions, of course, apply in and reasonably near to the ports. The times given in the tables are in Zone Time, that used being usually that corresponding with the Standard Time of the place in question. The Zone Times used are printed on every page of the tables and, in the case of Secondary Ports, the "time differences" given (see next page), when applied to the figures tabulated for the appropriate Standard Port, will give the times of H.W. and L.W. at the Secondary Port *in the Zone Time used for the Secondary Port*. This is not always the same as that used for the Standard Port. Zone G.M.T. is at present (1977) used for ports in the British Isles. Appendix 1 is part of the table for Walton on the Naze 1977.

Example. Required the times and heights in metres of H.W. and L.W. of the afternoon ebb tide at Walton on the Naze on 20th April, 1977. Also its duration and range.

From Appendix I: H.W.   1253   Height   4·1 m

                   L.W.   1852   Height   0·5 m

Duration   0559   Range   3·6 m

Secondary Ports. Frequently, however, the little ship will be concerned with the secondary ports rather than the standard ones, which are, for the most part, big mercantile ports. The secondary ports, which are very numerous, are listed in **alphabetical order (together with the ports in Part I) in the general index at the end of the tables. Here they are numbered in the order in which they appear in Part II, so that** they can readily be found. Part II is in two separate sections, the first giving height data in metres and the second giving height data in feet. The exact geographical positions are given in latitude and longitude and the times and heights of H.W. and L.W. are given in terms of differences from the corresponding times and heights at a nearly standard port. These differences are by no means constant but often vary a good deal from H.W. to L.W. and also vary with the times and heights at the standard port in question. Look at Appendix 2, which is from both sections of Part II of the tables, and shows some of the secondary ports which are referred to Walton. Here the first column gives the index numbers of the ports, the next column the names, and the next two columns the positions. The four columns under the heading "time differences" give the differences from the times of H.W. and L.W. at Walton when these times are as stated in heavy type at the tops of the respective columns in the Walton "panel." Thus, for Brightlingsea there appears in the L.W. column headed $\frac{1100}{2300}$ the time difference +0004 while in the L.W. column headed $\frac{0500}{1700}$ and the time difference +0046 appears. This means that on days when L.W. at Walton is 1100 and 2300 the times of L.W. at Brightlingsea is 4 minutes later, *i.e.* at 1104 and 2304, while on days when L.W. at Walton in 0500 and 1700, L.W. at Brightlingsea is 46 minutes later, *i.e.* at 0546 and 1746. A similar method is used for heights: thus when H.W. ht. at Walton is 4·2 m (13·8 ft.), H.W. height at Brightlingsea is 0·8 m (2·6 ft.) more, while when H.W. height at Walton is 3·4 m (11·0 ft.) that at Brightlingsea is 0·4 m (1·6 ft.) more. The time and height differences on days when the times and heights at the standard port are intermediate between those given in the table, can be obtained by interpolation—nearly always interpolation by eye is good enough though, if you have a pocket calculator, you may find it actually easier to do the arithmetic for interpolation. Thus, for example, because in the six hours between 0500 and 1100, the L.W. time difference drops by 42 minutes (from +0046 to +0004), if L.W. at Walton occurs at 0730 (2½ hours after 0500), L.W. at Bright-lingsea will occur at $46 - \dfrac{2 \cdot 5 \times 42}{6} = 29$ minutes later, *i.e.* at 1759. In a great many cases interpolation is not necessary at all because the tide and height differences do not change enough to be worth considering in practice. Appendix 2 shows several typical cases. A glance along the line for the Sunk Head Tower shows that the time difference changes only negligibly (by only 2 and 4 minutes for the H.W. and L.W. differences, respectively) while the shifts in the H.W. and L.W. height differences are too small to show in the metre table, being only 0·2 and 0·1 of a foot respectively. In ordinary navigation practice, therefore, one would take the H.W. and L.W. times at the Sunk Head Tower as the same as at Walton (they never differ by more than 2 minutes) and take the H.W. and L.W. heights as less than at Walton by 0·3 m (0·8 ft.) and 0·1 m (0·2 ft.) respectively. One of the great advantages of the Admiralty Tide Tables is that one can see by a mere glance along a line of figures in Part II whether one needs to interpolate or not, and how much the error will be if one does not.

    Example. Required the times and heights, in metres, of the forenoon H.W. and the following afternoon L.W. at Brightlingsea on 16th April, 1977.

Walton	1030	4·0 m	1641	0·7 m
			(from Appendix 1)	
Brightlingsea diffs	+0024	+0·7 m	+0046	0·0 m
			(from Appendix 2)	

Brightlingsea	1054	4·7 m	1727	0·7 m

Note: The H.W. time difference increases 4 minutes between 0600 and 1200, and therefore increases 3 minutes in $4\frac{1}{2}$ hours. Hence the H.W. time difference is 0021+3=0024. In normal practice, of course, one would not interpolate as closely as this, but it is done above to show the method.

Rise and Fall. The height of tide at any time between H.W. and L.W. can be found for any British port by using the appropriate mean springs and neaps curves diagram which is provided at the beginning of the set of predictions for the appropriate standard port. Appendix 3 shows the diagram preceding the predictions for Walton on the Naze. The Spring and Neap Ranges are printed on the diagram in metres only, but in practice it is convenient, the first time any particular diagram is used, to add the values in feet (there are metre/feet and feet/metre conversion tables in the early pages of the Admiralty Tide Tables) and also to add the approximate mean of the two ranges, also in both metres and feet, to the diagram. These additions to the printed diagram for Walton are shown in Appendix 3. The reasons for doing this will be appreciated later. To use the diagram the information required is the range and the interval before or after H.W. If the range is near (or more than) the mean springs range, the upper curve is employed, using the interval scale at the top of the diagram and reading off a "factor" from one or other of the two identical side scales. Thus, using the upper curve, the factor for $2^h 20^m$ before H.W. is 0·6. If the range is near (or less than) the mean neaps range, the lower curve is used, using the interval scale at the bottom of the diagram and reading off the factor from the central scale under the lower curve. Thus, using the lower curve, the factor for $3^h 40^m$ after H.W. is 0·34. In either case the range of the tide in question, when multiplied by the factor, gives the height *above L.W. height*, so, by adding the L.W. ht. the height of the tide at the time is obtained. If the range is not near either the mean springs or neaps range but between them, it may be necessary to make two calculations of height, one using each curve, and interpolate between them on a basis of range. If, however, the factors from the two curves are nearly the same (as they often will be) and the range itself is not very big, the double calculation will be unnecessary for both calculations will give nearly enough the same answer. A.T.T. contains a multiplication table (called Table II), the use of which will be obvious, for multiplying range by factor, so that the actual working calculation to be done is very small indeed. A pocket calculator will also do the multiplication.

The diagram for any standard port can also be used in the same way for the secondary ports referred thereto in Part II of A.T.T. except, of course, that the predicted heights, times, and range *at the secondary port* are employed when using the diagram.

Example. Required the height of the tide in feet at Burnham on Crouch at 0755 G.M.T. on 10th April, 1977.

Walton	0349	13·1	1004	3·1
			Range=13·1—3·1=10	
Diffs Burnham	+0045	+4·0	+0051	+0·9
Burnham	0434	17·1	1055	4·0
			Range=17·1—4·0=13·1	

0755 is 3^h 21^m before H.W. Burnham so the spring factor is 0·4 and the neap factor is 0·44. Because the range of 10 ft. at Walton is half way between the spring and neap ranges there we use a factor half way between the spring and the neap factors, *i.e.* 0·42. (The convenience of adding the figures shown in writing in Appendix 3 will now be appreciated.) The height of the tide at Burnham is obtained by multiplying the range at Burnham by the factor 0·42 and adding the L.W. height at Burnham.

$$0·42 \times 13·1 = 5·5$$
$$\text{L.W. Ht.} = 4·0$$
$$\text{Height} = 9·2$$

Obviously close interpolation like this would not be done in practice and is only done here to show the method. A glance at the diagram shows the two factors are so close together that interpolation is not ordinarily necessary.

Double Tides. In a number of areas, one of which is the popular yachting area between Swanage and the Nab Tower, double tides are experienced. In the case of the area Swanage to the Nab Tower the double tides are caused by the tidal wave coming up the English Channel dividing at the Isle of Wight and sending a branch wave up Spithead. This is, therefore, a special case for which the methods of reduction to soundings so far described in this chapter are not appropriate. A.T.T. contains two special tables (Tables III and IIIa) one in metres and the other in feet, covering this area. Part of Table IIIa, which is the one in feet, is shown in Fig. 16.

TABLE IIIa

SWANAGE TO NAB TOWER

(To be used for finding intermediate heights in feet for places named)

Place	Height of H.W. at Portsmouth	HOURLY HEIGHTS ABOVE CHART DATUM AT THE PLACE													Height of L.W. at Portsmouth
		Hours before or after HIGH WATER AT PORTSMOUTH							Hours before or after LOW WATER AT PORTSMOUTH						
		3b.	2b.	1b.	H.W.	1a.	2a.	3a.	2b.	1b.	L.W.	1a.	2a.	3a.	
	ft.	ft.	ft.	ft.	ft.	ft.	ft.	ft.	ft.	ft.	ft.	ft.	ft.	ft.	ft.
SWANAGE	15·5	6·3	6·0		4·3	4·5	4·1	2·5	1·9	1·1	2·6	4·4	5·5	5·8	2·0
	14·0	5·4	5·2	4·9	4·8	4·0	4·7	3·5	3·1	2·5	3·2	4·4	5·1	5·3	4·0
	12·4	4·8	4·9		5·1	5·2	5·0	4·3	4·1	3·6	3·8	4·4	4·6	4·7	5·9
POOLE ENTRANCE	15·5	6·5	6·3	5·3	4·6	4·8	4·6	2·9	2·2	1·1	2·6	4·2	5·4	6·1	2·0
	14·0	5·4	5·4	5·1	5·1	5·1	4·8	3·7	3·2	2·5	3·0	4·0	4·8	5·2	4·0
	12·4	4·7	4·8	4·9	5·0	5·2	5·0	4·4	4·1	3·6	3·6	4·1	4·4	4·6	5·9
POOLE BRIDGE	15·5	7·1	7·1	6·2	5·2	5·2	5·5	4·3	4·0	2·2	1·9	3·6	5·2	6·4	2·0
	14·0	5·9	5·5	5·4	5·5	5·8	6·0	4·9	4·6	3·2	2·7	3·7	5·0	5·6	4·0
	12·4	4·8	5·0	5·3	5·7	6·0	5·8	5·1	4·9	4·2	3·8	4·2	4·9	5·0	5·9
BOURNEMOUTH	15·5	6·8	6·6	5·6	4·8	5·1	4·9	3·1	2·3	1·1	2·1	4·0	5·6	6·4	2·0
	14·0	5·4	5·6	5·3	5·3	5·2	5·0	3·8	3·3	2·5	2·7	3·8	4·7	5·1	4·0
	12·4	4·8	4·9	5·0	5·1	5·3	5·1	4·5	4·3	3·7	3·5	4·0	4·4	4·7	5·9
CHRIST-† CHURCH HARBOUR	15·5	5·8	5·8	4·8	4·2	4·8	3·7	2·4	2·2	1·6	1·2	3·1	4·4	5·2	2·0
	14·0	4·9	4·8	4·6	4·6	4·9	4·0	2·8	2·5	2·1	2·2	2·9	3·3	3·5	4·0
	12·4														5·9
FRESHWATER BAY	15·5	8·0	8·3	7·8	7·3	7·2	6·2	3·7	2·9	1·6	2·7	4·8	6·4	7·2	2·0
	14·0	7·1	7·4	7·3	7·2	7·1	6·3	4·7	4·1	3·1	3·5	4·8	5·9	6·5	4·0
	12·4	6·3	6·7	7·1	7·3	7·1	6·4	5·3	5·0	4·2	4·4	5·2	5·6	6·0	5·9
TOTLAND BAY	15·5	7·7	8·2	8·0	7·5	7·5	7·0	4·5	3·5	1·5	2·5	4·5	6·0	6·9	2·0
	14·0	6·8	7·4	7·6	7·5	7·3	6·8	5·2	4·6	3·1	3·5	4·7	5·6	6·2	4·0
						7·3								5·8	6·0	5·9

Note.—Area enclosed by pecked lines represents the period during which the tide stands, or during which a second high water may occur.
† Heights at Christchurch are for inside the bar; outside the bar, L.W. falls about 2 feet lower at Springs.

FIG. 16

In this table heights at 18 different places are directly tabulated for three different values of H.W. and L.W. heights at Portsmouth, in terms of the interval from H.W. or L.W. at Portsmouth. If the interval is between 3 hours before and 3 hours after H.W. Portsmouth the table is entered with the H.W. height nearest to the actual H.W. height at Portsmouth. If the interval is between 2 hours before and 3 hours after L.W. at Portsmouth the table is entered with the L.W. height nearest to the actual L.W. height at Portsmouth. In either case the height of tide at the place in question is read directly from the table. Interpolation both as respects heights at Portsmouth and interval can be done by eye if required but will seldom be necessary in practice.

Example. Required the height of the tide at Christchurch Harbour at 1125 on a day when there is a H.W. at Portsmouth at 0409 ht. 11·3 ft. and a L.W. at 0923 ht. 2·2 ft.

Interval 1125 − 0923 = 0202 after L.W. Portsmouth. L.W. ht. Portsmouth 2·2 ft.

Entering Fig. 16 for Christchurch Harbour with L.W. Portsmouth ht. of 2·0 ft. (extreme right hand column) we find in the column for 2 hours after Portsmouth L.W. the figure of 4·4. This is the height required.

Margin of Error. However carefully tides may be worked out there is always a liability to unavoidable error due to unpredictable variations—notably weather and barometric pressure variations. *Therefore never navigate your ship where calculation indicates you have just enough water and no more, but allow yourself a reasonable margin "for luck."* A practical sort of margin to allow in ordinarily good weather is about half a fathom. In rough weather a larger margin should be allowed because, of course, waves take the ship above and below the theoretically calculated sea surface level. In reducing to soundings, however, work with reasonable accuracy—to the nearest foot is good practice. If an unknown weather error has crept in, it cannot be helped. It is not likely to be much. The weather and barometer effects are more or less the obvious ones. A persistently low barometer tends to raise sea level and a persistently high one to lower it. Strong winds blowing for long periods in the direction of the tidal wave tend to increase tidal heights and make the times of H.W. early. Strong winds in the opposite directions tend to produce the contrary effects. The shallower and more land-constricted the waters are, the greater are these barometer and weather vagaries. In the Thames Estuary exceptional weather and barometer conditions have been known to cause as much as about a fathom departure from predicted heights, but in the English Channel it is very rare to experience a departure exceeding half a fathom.

WARNING. Most datums have been adjusted to L.A.T. in the tide tables but not all published Admiralty charts have yet (in 1976) been reissued with the necessary adjustments to soundings. In such cases Notices to Mariners drawing attention to this have been issued. *Care should be taken to consult these if working tides to a closeness of two or three feet. Error resulting from ignoring this will almost always be errors of over-estimates of the depth of water and therefore often dangerous.*

CHAPTER V

TIDAL STREAMS

A tidal stream is a horizontal movement of the sea, mainly caused by the changing difference in height of the sea surface produced by a tide wave as it travels along constricted channels. In open unobstructed oceans, such as in mid-Atlantic, where the total height of the tide wave is small, the tidal stream is negligible. When, however, the wave enters limiting or shallow seas, such as the English Channel for example, it piles up due to the increasing frictional effect of the coastlines and sea-bed, and accordingly increases in height. This produces an increasing tendency for the water ahead of the crest to flow away in front of it and the water behind to flow away in the opposite direction. Once such a flow has started, the inertia of the water tends to keep the stream going for a while after the force which initiated the movement has ceased. Accordingly the relation between a tidal stream and the tide wave which causes it is apt to be complex and depends enormously upon geographical conditions. It is, therefore, very important to distinguish between a tide and a tidal stream caused thereby, and to remember that their times may be, and usually are, widely different. *It is a common and serious error to assume that the times of high and low water correspond to slack water.*

Inshore and Offshore Streams. In small harbours and inlets the tidal stream in and close to the entrance commonly floods and ebbs in correspondence with the local times of rising and falling tide. The stream flows into the harbour during the rising tide and out of it during the falling tide, and slack water in the entrance usually occurs at the " stands " of high and low water. In most other cases, however, this is by no means true. For example, where the tide enters a large estuary or land-locked basin through a narrow neck, the tendency is for the water in the estuary or basin to stabilise at or about mean level. A considerable flow of water into or out of the basin occurs only when the level outside becomes markedly different from that inside. In such cases *maximum* stream in the entrance is to be expected at or about the times of high and low water outside, and slack water as often as not occurs at about half-tide. Again, in channels which are wide and extensive the tidal stream in the offing may be expected to be at its maximum strength near the times of high and low water on the coast. In general, in such channels—of which the English Channel is an example—the tidal stream clear of the coast commonly overruns the time of high water at the coast by about three hours.

Main British Tidal Streams. Because of the complexity of the relationship between tides and tidal streams, it is usually impossible to lay down any very accurate general time connection between the two. However, in the more or less enclosed waters around the British Isles, the main streams behave as though they were flowing to and from points of maximum range. On the British coast of the English Channel the point of maximum range is near Dungeness. When the tide is rising at this point, the main stream will be found flowing towards it, and when it is falling the main stream will be found flowing away from it. Similarly, in the Irish Sea the tidal streams flow towards or away from the neighbourhood of Liverpool in dependence upon the condition of tide there, while in the southern North Sea the tidal stream in the area south of Cromer appears to flow towards or away from the neighbourhood of the North Foreland in dependence upon the state of tide there.

Sources of Tidal Stream Information. Tidal Atlases. Pilot Books. For actual navigation the most important and accurate sources of tidal stream information are the Tidal Stream Tables to be found on the Charts and described in Chapter I (see Fig. 5). Wherever a projected passage lies near a position in such a table, the information given therein should be used in preference to any other information. For planning a passage, however, it is usually more convenient to

use a TIDAL STREAM ATLAS. The Admiralty POCKET TIDAL
STREAM ATLASES are handy in size and generally ideally
suited for little ship use. These atlases are available at low
cost for many areas, including the northern and southern
portions of the North Sea and the English Channel. Official
TIDAL STREAM CHARTS, consisting of small chartlets which can
be cut up and clipped together to form a pocket atlas, are also
published for a number of areas. Fig. 17 is a reproduction of
one page of the pocket Tidal Stream Atlas for the Thames
Estuary. In these atlases and tidal stream charts, the directions
and strengths of the tidal stream are given for each hour with
reference to the time of high water at one, and sometimes two,
reference Standard Ports—in the example illustrated, Sheerness
and Dover. The streams are represented by arrows on which
are printed two figures. One of these (the larger, of course),
is the rate of the stream for that hour at springs, and the other
is the rate of the stream for that hour at neaps, both rates being
given in tenths of a knot. On the inside cover of the Atlas
is a simple diagram (with instructions for its use) by means of
which, if accurate working is required, the rate on any tide can
be obtained from a knowledge of the spring and neap ranges at
the Standard Port and a knowledge of the range there for that
particular tide. The rate can also be calculated by multiplying
the mean of the spring and neap rates printed on the appropriate
arrow on a Pocket Tidal Atlas chartlet by the range of the tide
in question, and dividing by the mean of the spring and neap
ranges printed on the "rise and fall" diagram (see Appendix 3)
which precedes the predictions for the reference Standard Port
in the Tide Tables.

Example. The mean spring and neap ranges printed on the
"rise and fall" diagram for Sheerness in the Tide Tables
are 5·1 m and 3·3 m (=16·7 ft. and 10·8 ft.). The spring
and neap rates printed on a particular arrow on a chartlet
in the Pocket Tidal Atlas for 3 hours before H.W. Sheerness
are 22 and 15 tenths of a knot. What rate would you
expect there at that time on a tide on which the Sheerness
range was 14 ft.?

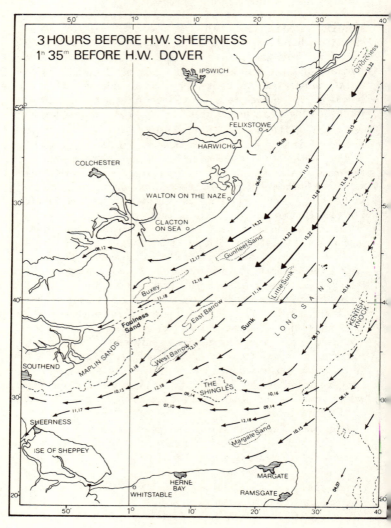

3 HOURS BEFORE H.W. SHEERNESS
1ʰ 35ᵐ BEFORE H.W. DOVER

Fɪɢ. 17.

Mean of the Sheerness ranges $=(16 \cdot 7 + 10 \cdot 8) \div 2$ $= 13 \cdot 8$
Mean of the two rates $\quad = (\ 2 \cdot 2 + \ 1 \cdot 5) \div 2$ $\ = \ 1 \cdot 85$
Expected rate $\quad\quad\quad = (14 \times 1 \cdot 85 \div 13 \cdot 8)$ $= \ 1 \cdot 9$
(very nearly)

The awkward arithmetic presents no difficulties to a pocket calculator. It will be noted, incidentally, that the above example provides another case in which the previous insertion, on a "rise and fall" diagram, of added metre and feet figures, such as are shown in Appendix 3, will be found useful.

Exactly the same method can be used for interpolating between spring and neap rates given on a chart for the "lettered" places thereon (see Fig. 5). For rough working, if only the spring rate is known, the neap rate may be assumed to be between half and two-thirds of it.

Co-tidal and Co-range Charts. These are charts on which are printed CO-TIDAL full lines and CO-RANGE pecked lines. Everywhere on a full line the time of H.W. differs from that at a reference Standard Port by the number of minutes printed on the line—*e.g.* —45 on a full line means that at all points along it H.W. is 45 minutes before that at the Standard Port. Everywhere along a pecked line has a range which is the same ratio (which is printed on the line) of the range at the Standard Port —*e.g.* 0·85 on a pecked line means that all points along it have a range equal to 0·85 of the range at the Standard Port. These ratios may also be taken as the ratios of the heights above datum at the Standard Port. Co-tidal and Co-range chartlets are sometimes included in Admiralty Pocket Tidal Atlases. They are invaluable for little ships navigating among sandbanks. For example, the one for the Thames Estuary (which is usually included in the Pocket Tidal Atlas for that area) has full lines at short intervals of time (most of them are 10 mins apart and some are only 5 mins apart); adjacent pecked lines have ratios differing by only 0·05; and two of the lines, one full and one pecked, go through the Wallet Spitway which, as East Coast yachtsmen know only too well, can often be identified by grounded yachts which have tried to pass through on the basis of insufficient tidal information.

For tidal streams of a purely local character, in the immediate neighbourhood of ports and so forth, the best sources of information are probably the official PILOT BOOKS. When approaching an unfamiliar harbour the information with regard to it in the appropriate Pilot should be read with care, especially the information relating to tides and tidal streams.

Accuracy of Tidal Stream Predictions. Although the information given by chart tidal stream tables, by tidal stream atlases, and by Pilots is, in general, remarkably accurate and adequate for seaman-like navigation if ordinary common-sense precautions are observed, it must be remembered that the reliability of a tidal stream prediction is unavoidably somewhat less than that of a tide prediction. This is because a tidal stream in narrow waters is more liable to unpredictable changes due to changing sandbanks, weather, winds, and so on.

Barometer and Weather Vagaries. Weather and barometer variations causing changes in tide heights will obviously also cause changes in tidal streams. These changes may manifest themselves as changes in the rates or in the duration of ebb and flow, or both. Thus a persistent anticyclone over the North Sea will tend to depress the general sea-level there and thereby cause a strengthening of the north-going stream (the ebb), back from the Foreland, at the expense of the flood stream. Similarly, a succession of deep low-pressures over the Channel will tend to raise the level there and strengthen the east-going stream (the flood), towards Dungeness, at the expense of the ebb stream. Persistent strong winds also tend to modify tidal streams. Such winds tend to blow the water not quite directly before them, but about two points to starboard in the northern hemisphere or about two points to port in the southern. Thus, in home waters, a strong persistent west wind will tend, of itself, to produce a stream setting about ESE, assuming, of course, that the land configuration allows of it. In the main channels round our coasts, changes in streams due to wind action are generally small and rarely, if ever, exceed 1 knot, but in narrower and shallower waters these effects may easily be well marked.

Local Variations of Tidal Streams. There are many local

tidal stream variations of a general nature which are well worth remembering, and which can often be turned to the navigator's advantage, especially the navigator under sail. Thus, the tidal stream along a bay-indented coastline spreads into bays, with the result that the stream is nearly always markedly slacker inside a bay than outside in the general channel. Similarly the rate of a stream usually increases locally near a headland to a value well above the average elsewhere, tricky and sometimes dangerous eddies often occurring close against the upstream side of the headland. Fig. 18 illustrates this action, the nature of which is fairly obvious. If, therefore, considerations of safety allow, the " sting " of a foul tide can often be much reduced by working well into bays, though if the stream is still foul when a bay has been traversed, the next headland should be well cleared, otherwise the ship will lose off the headland as much or more than she has gained in the bay.

Insets. There is almost always a substantial inset of a

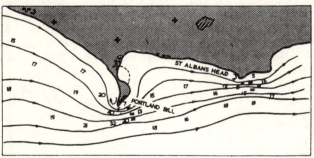

FIG. 18.

stream into a bay or bight. In general, the bigger the bay the more the inset. In thick weather the navigator should beware of this effect and should allow for an inset whether or not he has positive information as to its existence.

Races and Overfalls. If soundings change sharply, the effect of a fast tidal stream in passing over the " step " on the sea bottom often causes a more or less serious disturbance or turmoil of water on the surface. This is also shown in

Fig. 18 (note the races off Portland and St. Albans Head and

FIG. 19.

the soundings in their neighbourhoods) and in Fig. 19, which perhaps better illustrates the action. Such disturbances are known as RACES or OVERFALLS, and usually occur a little "downstream" of the "step." If they are serious enough to be marked on a chart they are, at best, uncomfortable for a little ship, and probably dangerous to her. *There is really only one safe rule for races and overfalls—keep away.* Seamen with much local knowledge may, and do, "take liberties" with a race in their "own back garden," but it is foolhardy and unseamanlike for a stranger to attempt it. Especially is this so when under sail, for a change in wind force or direction may mean being carried into a race at a dangerous time. In most cases a comparatively small detour is enough to ensure both safety and comfort. Wherever the chart shows a sharp change in soundings an awkward sea is likely to be experienced, even in moderate winds, when the tidal stream is running fast, especially if the stream is meeting the wind.

Large Harbours and Estuaries. The navigator should beware of comparatively sudden changes in direction and strength of a tidal stream near large harbours, estuary entrances, and so on. Refer back to Fig. 17, which illustrates this type of action admirably. Observe the separation of tidal streams by the Buxey, the Shingles and off the N. Foreland.

Cheating Tidal Streams. By carefully planning a passage in advance with the aid of charts such as that reproduced in Fig. 17, and by the use of a little common sense, a navigator can often "cheat" a stream quite effectively. For example, by standing inshore before the end of a foul stream, advantage may be taken of the fact that the in-shore stream will in most cases have turned some hours before, and by sailing out again before a fair stream inshore turns foul, advantage may be taken of the fact that the offing stream will be running fair for some time. In this way, in the English Channel a fair stream may often be carried for seven or eight hours and a foul stream reduced to only four or five.

Rough-and-Ready Estimation. If the only information about a tidal stream is the spring rate, the speed at any other condition of moon may be roughly estimated by assuming it to be equal to the spring rate for the hour in question multiplied by the ratio of the range for the day to the spring range. Also, in the absence of any better information, a flood or ebb stream may be assumed to flow for six hours and to run at one-third its maximum rate in the first and last hours, two-thirds in the second, and fifth hours, and the full rate in the third and fourth hours.

Caution. In approaching a harbour take every precaution to observe, by the use of shore marks, the tidal stream that is actually occurring as you approach, *especially if you do not know the times of high and low water at that harbour*. If the stream is running fast in the offing the probabilities are that it will be near high or low water inside, and in the latter case if the entrance is shallow the obvious precautions will have to be taken. *Do not assume that a fast stream in the offing means half tide in the entrance—the opposite is more probably true.* Remember that, in a narrow channel with a fast flood or ebb tide, there is usually a slight set towards the sides during the flood stream and a slight set away from them during the ebb. Remember also that, in shoal-filled waters (such, for example, as the Thames Estuary), where the depths over banks increase from little or nothing at low tide, the local tidal stream directions are likely to change rapidly from hour to hour, and to differ considerably from place to place at the same time. *Therefore, especially when navigating such waters without the aid of a detailed tidal stream chart, watch the effects of the streams carefully by any marks that are available, and do not steer by eye but always set compass courses where possible.* This point will be elaborated more fully later.

CHAPTER VI

NAVIGATIONAL INSTRUMENTS: THE MAGNETIC COMPASS

The principle of the magnetic compass is so much a part of common knowledge as to warrant only the most brief description here.   If a magnetised bar is free to swing in a horizontal plane it will set itself to lie along the lines of the earth's magnetic field, which run approximately, though not quite directly, between the N and S magnetic poles.   If, therefore, such a bar is pivoted about a vertical axis and attached to a circular card having its edge marked, for example, in degrees, and a pointer fixed in or parallel to the fore-and-aft line of a ship is mounted to read against the card's edge, its reading will indicate the angle between the direction of the earth's magnetic field and the direction of the fore-and-aft line.

Lubber's Line.   This is illustrated in Fig. 20, which shows a

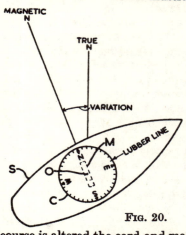

MAGNETIC N

TRUE N

VARIATION

LUBBER LINE

M

m

S

O

C

Fig. 20.

card C attached to a magnetised bar M pivoted at O so that it can swing in a horizontal plane.   The co-operating pointer, or LUBBER'S LINE, as it is called, is fixed in or parallel to the fore-and-aft line of the ship, being in practice incorporated in the housing of the compass.   Provided there is no other magnetic interference, the bar M sets itself so that its north-seeking end always points to the magnetic N.   If the ship's course is altered the card and magnet " stay put," the lubber's

66

line rotating with the ship round the card and reading directly the angle between the direction of ship's head and the direction of magnetic N.   In Fig. 20 the ship is headed a little N of E.

Variation and Deviation.   As already explained in Chapter I, the VARIATION—the angle between magnetic N and true N—varies from place to place and also varies with time, but can be readily ascertained for any time and place from the chart. It will be obvious from Fig. 20 that if anything magnetic is placed near the compass so as to provide local attraction or so as locally to distort the earth's magnetic field, it may deviate the compass away from magnetic N and thereby introduce an error called DEVIATION.   This will be dealt with more fully in the next chapter.

Dead-Beat Liquid Compasses.   Clearly, the practical utility of a compass depends upon the ability of its magnet to remain steady on the north point despite the rolling and pitching of the ship in which it is mounted.   For many years this constituted an only partly solved problem for the compass designer.   Nowadays, however, this problem is, practically speaking, fully solved by the so-called DEAD-BEAT LIQUID COMPASS, which is the only really satisfactory type for little ship use.   In this type of compass a system of short, powerful magnets—usually at least four—mounted parallel to one another in a light frame, replaces the single magnet of Fig. 20, and is attached to a card pivoted in a bowl filled with a mixture of rectified spirits and distilled water.   This liquid mixture serves to damp out the undesired swinging and oscillating movements which would otherwise occur due to the motion of the ship in a seaway.

Compass Cards.   There are three main types of compass card in common use, differing from one another only in the way in which their edge markings divide the circle.   These three types are illustrated concentrically within one another in Fig. 21.   Here the outermost ring shows the circular notation type of card, the middle ring the quadrantal type, and the inner ring the points type.   These three rival notation systems have already been described in Chapter I, in connection with compass roses on charts.   The choice between the three types of card is very much a matter of personal opinion. In the author's view, however, the circular notation card is generally much to be preferred, though it has one defect (sometimes, admittedly, a fatal one), that the degree markings may be by no means easy for the helmsman to see,

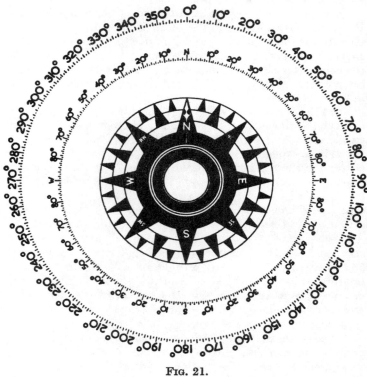

FIG. 21.

so that steering may be made very fatiguing. There are, however, excellent compass card magnifying lenses available— sometimes incorporated as part of the compass structure and sometimes provided as an extra fitting for attachment— which will usually suffice to overcome this disadvantage.

Plate II shows one common form of magnifier attachment. If, in any particular ship, it is practicable to mount a compass having a card of 5 inches or more in diameter, so that degree markings can be clearly and comfortably seen by the helmsman (if necessary with the aid of a magnifier), the selection of this type of card is recommended. If, however, this is not possible, the points type of card should be selected. It is a good deal easier on the helmsman's eye than the circular notation card, but the divisions are inconvenient from the navigator's point of view, since they divide the circle into 32 points, each of 11¼ degrees. The quadrantal type of card has, in the author's opinion, nothing to commend it for little ship use. Its markings are as difficult to see and steer by as those of the circular notation card, while it does not possess the logical simplicity of the latter card, with its sensible division of the circle into 360 degrees numbered consecutively clockwise. A conversion table for inter-converting the three types of notation is included in the appendix section of this book for the convenience of those who may have a points or quadrantal compass already installed.

Parallax. A minor defect of any compass in which a lubber's line is used to read against the card edge is that, unless the helmsman is directly behind the compass so as to have his eye in one straight line with the centre of the card and the lubber's line, there is a liability to an error of observation called PARALLAX. This will be clear from Fig. 22. A compass card C and lubber's line L in the relative positions shown in this figure will appear correctly to a helmsman with his eye at X, directly behind the compass, but if, as in practice often happens, the helmsman's position is to one side, he will receive a false impression. If his eye is, for example, at Y, the lubber's line will appear to the left of the N point when in fact it is as shown. The result will be that, unless parallax is allowed for, the wrong course will be steered. In practice parallax is easily estimated and allowed for by putting the ship correctly on course with the eye directly behind the compass, and then moving quickly over to the normal steering position, noting how the compass then appears and steering accordingly. Nevertheless, parallax is a decided nuisance even with a careful and experienced helmsman, and is apt to be forgotten under sail, where a change of tacks may bring the helmsman from one side of the compass to the other with a consequent reversal of the direction of parallax error.

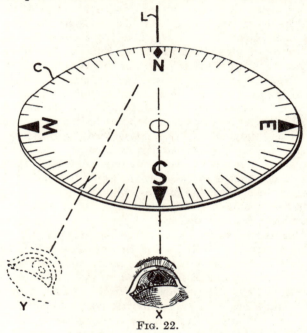

FIG. 22.

Another defect, perhaps more important, of the ordinary lubber's line type of compass, is that to steer a course in some direction between the larger marks on the card—*e.g.* to a degree marking between the 5° lines on a circular notation card or to one of the quarter point markings on a points card— imposes a considerable strain on the helmsman and is, indeed, often impossible in a seaway. Accordingly the navigator may be compelled to order a course some way off the best course merely to make it easier for the helmsman.

Grid Steering Compass. A type of compass which avoids both these defects, having practically no parallax error and enabling a course to be set to a degree while at the same time imposing no eye-strain or need for thought on the helmsman, is the GRID STEERING COMPASS. This type, which was originally developed for aircraft and is very widely used in the air, has much to commend it for little ship use. One excellent modern example, designed to be fixed to the cabin deck head or suspended from a shelf in the cockpit, is shown in Plate III. This example is of the inverted type with an adjustable mirror R in which the reflection of the compass proper is seen and which can be set to suit the helmsman's convenience. The bottom of the compass proper consists of a window W which can be rotated into, and clamped in, any position of adjustment, and which carries a ring N marked in circular notation and a T-like pattern of lines T. There is no card as ordinarily understood, but instead, the magnet system carries so-called grid wires with three thin luminous lines G corresponding to the N, E, and W points, the N point being distinguished by being crossed. The luminous lines G also form a T which can be brought into the position shown in Plate III centrally within the T pattern on the window. To set a course with this compass, the navigator rotates the window W so that the required course is indicated by a pointer P against an edge scale S on the window frame, and clamps it there. Thereafter, all the helmsman has to do is to steer so as to keep the grid lines G inside and parallel to the T on the window. The eye is very sensitive to departures from parallelism and a departure of as little as 1° from the desired course is instantly and plainly apparent. The helmsman has no figures or point markings to observe and, indeed, does not even need to know the course, while all the navigational advantages of the circular notation are retained. A luminous compass of this type is excellent for night work and external lighting seldom has to be used, except perhaps in periods of " half light," when the luminous material may not show up well. The principal defects of the grid steering compass are that, unless it be of the reflector type (such as that illustrated), the helmsman must look down on it, so it must be installed low—which is not always convenient; it takes a little getting used to, since the T on the window is in a different radial position for each different course; and it does not readily lend itself to taking bearings—it is essentially a steering compass. The last point is seldom of importance in practice, since more often than not it is impossible anyway to instal the steering compass of a little ship in such a position as to give the all-round view required for taking bearings.

Compass Installation. The ideal requirements for the installation of a compass to be used both for steering and taking bearings are easily stated and usually impossible to satisfy in a little ship. They are: (1) freedom from magnetic interference; (2) convenience to the helmsman whether sitting to windward or to lee on either tack; and (3) a good all-round view. In most little ships it is necessary to begin by discarding all hopes of satisfying (3), reserving the ship's compass for steering and carrying a hand bearing compass for bearings. As regards (1) and (2), a compromise must nearly always be struck. Freedom from magnetic interference involves that the compass should be as far as possible from large masses of iron, common examples of which are iron keels, auxiliary or other engines, and funnels in motor ships. It also involves that the compass shall be remote from any other compass and from electrical sources of magnetic interference, of which, probably, the most troublesome are dynamos, such as battery-charging dynamos, which may perhaps introduce no deviation when not switched on (when the compass adjuster is aboard to adjust the compass) and most serious deviation when running. Beware of dynamos and also of some ignition coils, which can also introduce unsuspected errors. In general a reasonable compromise between requirements (1) and (2) can be struck, but in some cases satisfactory freedom from interference leaves the compass in a by no means convenient position. In such a case it is quite a good dodge to carry an extra in the form of a small grid steering compass mounted on gimbals in a portable box fitted with hooks to enable it to be hooked on to the cockpit coaming in any position on either side. Hook the " extra " wherever is most convenient to the helmsman—just in front of his chosen steering position in the windward corner of the cockpit, for example—and while he is uncomfortably holding the ship on the chosen course by the ship's compass, set the grid of the extra to read " on course." He can then take up his comfortable position and steer by the extra so long as that course is required.   Of course the extra compass must not be put near the ship's compass. When the course is changed or it is required to move the extra to the other side of the cockpit, set it up again in the same way. If the extra compass is of the luminous type, this dodge enables the ship's compass lighting to be kept switched off most of the night.

Hand Bearing Compass. A most useful and frequently essential adjunct to the well-found little ship is a hand bearing compass, a first rate example of which is the Mini-Compass (Offshore Instruments Ltd) shown in Plate I. It is perfectly dead beat and very robust, though weighing only about 4 ounces and measuring only about 3 ins. diameter by $1\frac{1}{2}$ ins. thick. The body is a rubber encircled Tritium gas sealed capsule which incorporates a magnifying prism through which the edge of the compass card and the object whose bearing is being taken can be viewed simultaneously, with the object seen directly against the scale, so that there is no parallax error.   The card is of the 360° type with a separate line for each degree and these lines appear well separated, thanks to the optical magnification provided.   The compass is self-illuminated—*i.e.* no battery and bulb are needed—and can be easily read by day or at night so that the trouble that now afflicts the once popular electrically lit type of hand bearing compass, namely that it is difficult nowadays to obtain non-magnetic battery cells, is avoided. For all practical purposes a hand bearing compass, if intelligently used, can be regarded as free from deviation.   It is necessary, however, always to take stock of your own personal position when using it.   If you use it to take a bearing while leaning over the engine casing, or holding it close over the ship's compass, or steadying yourself by a steel wire shroud with the hand bearing compass up against the wire—all of which have been known to happen—the results obtained may be more surprising than reliable.

CHAPTER VII

THE COMPASS: CORRECTING AND CHECKING

True and Magnetic Courses and Bearings. A course or bearing as given by a magnetic compass will differ from a true course or bearing by the angle of the variation, assuming there is no magnetic interference with the compass due to ironwork in the ship. A course or bearing, obtained from the chart with reference to true N, is a TRUE COURSE or BEARING. When corrected by applying the variation, it becomes a MAGNETIC COURSE or BEARING. If the variation is westerly, a compass not subjected to magnetic interference will point to W of true N. If the variation is easterly the compass will point to E of true N. The amount of the variation is always given in degrees: variation 10° W means that a magnetic compass, free of interference, points its magnet system 10° W of true N.

Deviation. In practice, however, it frequently happens that a compass is not free from magnetic interference. In such a case the N-seeking end of the magnet system no longer points to the magnetic N, but is deflected away from it, either E or W, by an amount depending on the interference. As will be seen later, this interference varies with every ship and is, moreover, not constant in any particular ship, but depends upon the direction in which the ship's head is pointed, so that the deflection away from magnetic N is easterly on some courses and westerly on others. The angle by which the magnetic system of a compass is deflected or deviated, by interference, away from magnetic N is called the DEVIATION, and, like variation, its amount is stated in degrees E or W.

Compass Error. Compass Courses and Bearings. It will now be seen that a course or bearing as indicated by a compass differs from a true course or bearing by two factors, variation and deviation, either or both of which may be E or W. The sum of these factors, combined with due regard as to whether each is E or W, is called the ERROR of the compass. A true course or bearing, when corrected for the error—that is to say, by applying both variation and deviation—becomes a COMPASS COURSE or COMPASS BEARING. Clearly, variation and deviation, when of opposite names (one E and one W) tend to cancel one another out; if both are E or both are W, they reinforce one another to increase the error. Fig. 23 illustrates a case where the total error is 15° W, made up of 10° W variation and 5° W deviation (the latter being due, probably, to the auxiliary engine G).

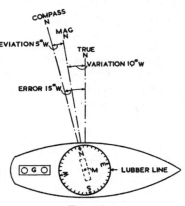

FIG. 23.

Correction of Courses and Bearings. The conversion of true courses and bearings into compass courses and bearings, and vice versa, is one of the commonest tasks of the navigator, and if a regular method of working is not adopted, it is distressingly easy to make mistakes by applying variation or deviation the wrong way. The problem presents itself in practice in one of two forms: either (1) it is required to convert a true course or bearing, taken from the chart, into a compass course or bearing for use by the helmsman; or (2) it is required to convert a course or bearing, taken with the compass, into true for laying off on the chart. *It is strongly recommended to do all chart work in true and all conversion calculations in circular* (360°) *notation.* If this be done, the same simple, easily memorised rule for applying variation and deviation always holds good whether you are working from the chart to the compass or from the compass to the chart. This rule is:

Anything west
compass is best;
Anything east
compass is least.

Suppose it is required to lay off on the chart a bearing of S 30° E, taken by a compass with quadrantal markings, variation being 10° W and deviation 7° E. *Begin by converting to circular notation.* Then apply variation and deviation by the above rule. S 30° E is 150° in circular notation. 7° E and 10° W combine to make an error of 3° W. *Anything west compass is best.* The compass reading (150) must therefore, in this case, be " best," *i.e.* the greater. The corrected, true, bearing is therefore 150−3=147°. Since the true compass rose on the chart is in circular notation, this can now be laid off direct.

Exactly the same rule applies in working from " true " to " compass." Suppose a true course of 016° is taken from the chart, variation being 10° W and deviation 4° W. These combine to make an error of 14° W. *Anything west compass is best.* The required compass course is therefore 016+14 =030°. You may now convert this into whatever notation your compass uses. If it is a circular notation compass no conversion is necessary, of course. If it is a compass with quadrantal markings 030°=N 30° E; for a compass with point markings 030°=NE by N ¼ N (to the nearest quarter point).

Example 1. With variation 9° W and deviation 11° E, correct a compass bearing of N by E, obtained by a compass with point markings, into a true bearing for the chart.

N by E=011° (to the nearest degree).
Error (9° W and 11° E)=2° E.
True bearing (*anything east compass is least*)=011+2 =013°.

Example 2. With variation 9° W and deviation 14° E, correct a true course of 340° into a compass course for a compass with quadrantal markings.

Error (9° W and 14° E)=5° E.

Compass course (*anything east compass is least*)=340−5
=335°.

335° converted into quadrantal notation is N 25° W.

If the compass has no deviation (as, in practice, is always assumed for a hand bearing compass, and will be the case, at any rate on certain courses, for the ship's compass), a compass course or bearing becomes the same as a magnetic course or bearing. The same rule still applies, because deviation is now zero and the error consists merely of the variation.

Example 3. With variation 13° W, convert a true course of 212° into a magnetic course in quadrantal notation.

Error=13° W.

Magnetic course (*anything west compass is best*)=212+13
=225=S 45° W.

Example 4. With variation 11° W, convert a magnetic bearing of SE, taken by a hand bearing compass with points markings (no deviation), into a true bearing for the chart.

SE is 135° in circular notation.

Error=11° W.

True bearing (*anything west compass is best*)=135−11
=124°.

Change of Deviation with Ship's Head. As mentioned above, the deviation in any particular ship is not constant but depends upon the direction in which the ship's head is pointed. The reason for this will be seen from Fig. 24, which illustrates a ship wherein deviation is caused by an auxiliary engine G. Suppose the engine attracts the N-seeking end of the magnet system and is installed directly abaft the compass. In Fig. 24 (*a*) the ship is headed N magnetic, the engine is, therefore, in line with the compass pivot in the direction N magnetic, and there is no deflecting effect on the magnet system, which is represented in the figure by the single needle

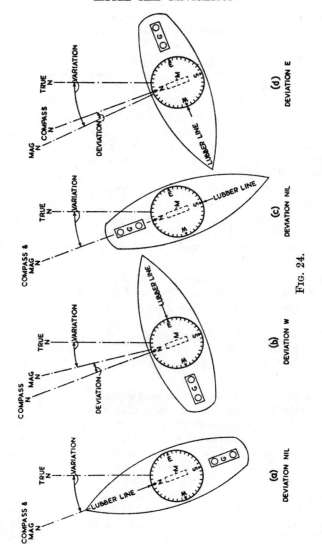

FIG. 24.

M shown dotted. Compass N and magnetic N are therefore the same. In Fig. 24 (*b*), however, in which the ship is headed E by compass, the engine G and needle M are so positioned in relation to one another, that the former can exert maximum attraction on the latter to deflect it W, and there is, accordingly, maximum W deviation. In Fig. 24 (*c*) the ship is headed S by compass, the engine and compass pivot are again in the N magnetic line, and deviation is again nil. In Fig. 24 (*d*), with the ship headed W by compass, the engine G is to the E of the compass, and in a position to produce maximum E deviation. As the ship's head is changed from (*a*) to (*b*), W deviation gradually increases to a maximum; from (*b*) to (*c*), W deviation decreases again to zero; from (*c*) to (*d*), E deviation increases to a maximum; and from (*d*) round to (*a*) again, E deviation falls away to zero. A similar result would clearly be obtained wherever the engine G was installed except that, if it were not directly abaft or directly forward of the compass, the courses with zero deviation would not be magnetic N and S, but two other courses 180° apart.

Compass Adjustment. When a compass is installed in a ship the deviations for the different directions of ship's head should be ascertained, and reduced as much as possible by fixing small compensating magnets and pieces of iron in the compass stand in the proper positions to compensate for the undesired magnetic interference and thus adjust the compass. This adjustment process is a task which is best undertaken by a compass-adjuster, and the compensating magnets and parts positioned by him should not be moved or otherwise tampered with. It frequently happens that when the compass has been adjusted, some deviation still remains. This does not matter so long as it is not too large *and so long as the amount of the deviation on any course is known so that it can be allowed for*. In general, in a little ship, a maximum deviation exceeding 5° or 6° or so should not be tolerated. If, on any course, the deviation is found to exceed this value, the compass adjuster should be called in and the compass re-adjusted.

Deviation Table. The deviation of the compass is recorded in a DEVIATION TABLE, which should be written out on a card,

varnished or otherwise protected against the weather, and
kept handy to the navigator. The deviation table may take
any of a variety of different forms, but the most convenient
is a three-column table, of which the middle column gives

Ship's Head Compass	Deviation	Ship's Head Magnetic
N	6° E	006
N by E	7°	018
NNE	8°	030
NE by N	8°	042
NE	8°	053
NE by E	7°	063
ENE	6°	074
E by N	5°	084
E	4°	094
E by S	3°	104
ESE	1°	114
SE by E	Nil	124
SE	1° W	134
SE by S	3°	143
SSE	4°	153
S by E	5°	164
S	6°	174
S by W	7°	184
SSW	8°	194
SW by S	8°	206
SW	8°	217
SW by W	7°	229
WSW	6°	242
W by S	5°	254
W	4°	266
W by N	3°	278
WNW	2°	290
NW by W	Nil	304
NW	2° E	317
NW by N	3°	329
NNW	4°	341
N by W	5°	354

FIG. 25.

deviation, and the two outer columns the corresponding
directions of ship's head by compass and ship's head magnetic.
The column headed " Ship's head by compass " should be
prepared in whatever form of notation (circular, quadrantal,
or points) the compass uses. Common practice is to prepare

the column " Ship's head magnetic " in quadrantal notation, but in the author's opinion it is more convenient to prepare this column in circular notation, since it will be wanted only when working from chart to compass, and a course taken from the chart will always be in circular notation if the practice recommended herein is followed. Fig. 25 is a typical example of such a three-column table prepared for use in a ship whose compass is marked in points notation. With such a table, correction of courses and bearings is extremely easy.

Example 1. With variation 10° W and using the table of Fig. 25, what is the compass course corresponding to a true course of 143°?

True course 143°.

Variation 10° W.

Magnetic course (*anything west compass is best*; and we are working *from* chart *to* compass)=153°.

Compass course (read straight from the table, since 153° is tabulated)=SSE.

Example 2. With variation 10° W and using the table of Fig. 25, what is the compass course corresponding to a true course of 099°?

True course 099°.

Magnetic course (*anything west compass is best*)=109°.

Deviation (interpolating between 104° and 114° in table)=2° E.

Compass course (*anything east compass is least*)=109−2 =107°=E by S ½ S (to the nearest quarter point).

Example 3. With variation 10° W and using the table of Fig. 25, convert a compass bearing of N by W, taken when the ship was heading SW by compass, into a true bearing for the chart.

N by W in circular measure is 349 (to nearest degree).

Variation=10° W.

Deviation (for heading SW by compass)=8° W.

Error=10 W+8 W=18° W.

True bearing (*anything west compass is best*)=349−18 =331°.

CAUTION.—When correcting bearings *beware of taking the deviation for the bearing instead of that for the ship's head.* This is an obvious but common slip. If, in Example 3 above, we had taken the deviation for the bearing (N by W) instead of that for the ship's head (SW), we should have used a deviation of 5° E instead of 8° W, involving an error of 13°.

Swinging Ship. Although the adjustment of the compass is a matter for the expert, ascertaining the deviation on different courses and making a deviation table is not. The deviation on any particular course can be found by steadying the ship carefully on that course and taking a bearing of some object whose true bearing is known. Then apply the variation to the true bearing and compare the compass bearing with the correct magnetic bearing thus obtained. The difference is the deviation, which will be E if the compass bearing (in circular notation) is least (smaller), or W if the compass is best. The process of obtaining a deviation table by comparing a series of compass bearings, obtained on different courses, with a known bearing is called SWINGING SHIP. Swinging ship may be done at anchor, hauling the ship round her hook, or, if this is inconvenient, she may be got under way and steamed round in a circle, and steadied on the successive required courses. It will be clear that the ship should be, as nearly as possible, in the same position each time a bearing is taken, and therefore if she is steamed round in a circle, it should be as " tight " as possible, so that the diameter is negligibly small as compared to the distance away of the object observed. This distance should be two or three miles if possible. It is probably best to take advantage of two shore objects whose bearing, when in line, is given on the chart. The usual practice is to take bearings when the ship is headed on the cardinal and inter-cardinal points, namely N, NE, E, SE, S, SW, W, and NW. Strictly speaking, the ship should be headed N, NE, E, etc., *magnetic*, but it is much easier to head the ship on these directions *by compass* and the error introduced by so doing is, for practical purposes, negligible. An example of swinging ship is given below.

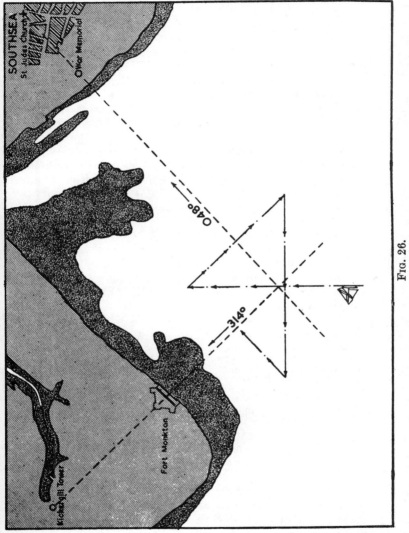

Fig. 26.

Example. A yacht in Spithead on a calm day decides to swing ship to obtain a deviation table for her compass, which has quadrantal markings. From the chart (see Fig. 26) it is seen that St. Jude's Church, Southsea, and the War Memorial, in line, bear 048°. It is also seen that this line crosses a line, bearing 314°, through Kickergill Tower and the centre of Fort Monckton. The yacht is accordingly steered so as repeatedly to cross the War Memorial–St. Jude's line, being steadied each successive time on the courses N, NE, E, SE, etc., by compass, and a bearing of the Memorial is taken each time these objects come into line. A glance is taken, just before each crossing of the line, to see that Kickergill Tower is also more or less in line with the centre of Fort Monckton. Since this line makes a good angle (about a right angle) with the War Memorial line, this will ensure that the yacht is approximately in the same position each time a bearing is taken. The variation is 10° W. The bearings obtained are as shown by columns 1 and 3 below. Obtain a deviation table by filling in the remaining columns.

True bearing, 048°. Variation 10° W. Correct magnetic bearing, 058°.

Column 1 Ship's Head by Compass	Column 2 Ship's Head in Circular Notation	Column 3 Compass Bearing	Column 4 Compass Bearing in Circular Notation	Column 5 Correct Magnetic Bearing	Column 6 Deviation
N	000 °	N 52° E	052°	058°	6° E
NE	045°	N 50° E	050°	058°	8° E
E	090°	N 54° E	054°	058°	4° E
SE	135°	N 59° E	059°	058°	1° W
S	180°	N 64° E	064°	058°	6° W
SW	225°	N 66° E	066°	058°	8° W
W	270°	N 62° E	062°	058°	4° W
NW	315°	N 56° E	056°	058°	2° E

Checking Observations. When deviations have been obtained as above described the accuracy of the observations can be checked by adding the deviations obtained on the

courses N, E, S, and W, with due regard to whether they are
E or W, and similarly adding those obtained on the courses
NE, SE, SW, and NW. These two sums should, theoretically,
give the same answer, but there will usually be a difference
of one or two degrees—in the above example, one degree.
A small difference like this can be ignored for it involves an
error of only $\frac{1}{4}°$, but if the difference is 8° or 10° or more,
something is wrong.

Lubber's Line Error. The observations can also be used to
check whether the compass has been properly installed with
the lubber's line correctly fore-and-aft. Add together, with
due regard to whether they are E or W, the deviations obtained
on courses N, S, E, and W. The sum should be zero. If it
is not, divide it by 4, and the answer is the amount by which
the compass is twisted out of its correct position. If the sum
is E the deviation due to this cause (which will be the same
on all courses) is E; if the sum is W the deviation due to this
cause is W. The compass in the above example was correctly
installed.

Intermediate Courses. Having obtained the deviations for
eight directions of ship's head, make a graph of them by
plotting the deviations against ship's head on squared or ruled
paper. Then draw a smooth curve through the plots. Fig. 27
shows such a curve drawn for the observations in the above
example. The curve should be, as shown, a symmetrical
" wave " which crosses the zero deviation line at points
180° apart. Deviations for other intermediate directions of
ship's head can be read off from it to complete a table like that
of Fig. 25, with deviation given for each point of the compass,
or each 10°, as may be required.

In Fig. 27 the measured deviations are indicated by crosses
and the intermediate deviations, which are taken from the
curve to complete the table of Fig. 25, are indicated by
encircled dots.

Obtaining Deviation when Correct Shore Bearing not Known.
If the correct bearing of a shore mark is not ascertainable
from the chart, that mark may still be used for swinging ship,
because its correct magnetic bearing is (so nearly as not to

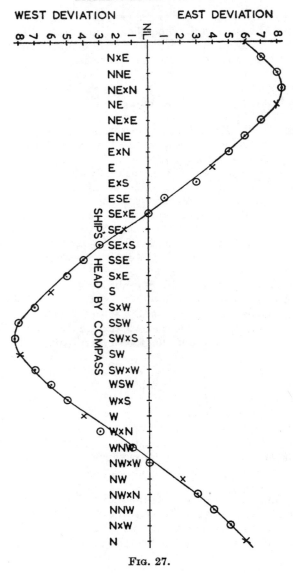

Fig. 27.

matter) the average of the bearings taken on eight equally spaced courses. Suppose that, in the previous example, the true bearing of the War Memorial was not known, but the ship had nevertheless been swung, as illustrated in Fig. 26, on the courses N, NE, E, etc. The eight bearings obtained were :

$$
\begin{array}{r}
\text{N } 52° \text{ E} \\
\text{N } 50° \text{ E} \\
\text{N } 54° \text{ E} \\
\text{N } 59° \text{ E} \\
\text{N } 64° \text{ E} \\
\text{N } 66° \text{ E} \\
\text{N } 62° \text{ E} \\
\text{N } 56° \text{ E} \\
\hline
8)463 \\
\hline
\end{array}
$$

N 58° E (very nearly).

The average of the eight bearings is (very nearly) 058°—the same as was obtained from the chart. Thus, in the example of Fig. 26 the War Memorial, St. Jude's Church, Kickergill Tower, and Fort Monckton could all be used as described, even though you did not know their names or what their correct bearings were. Deviation can also be obtained by taking compass bearings of a heavenly body and comparing them with the known correct bearings of the body at the time. The compass-adjuster generally uses the sun.

Pelorus. If the compass has no sighting vane or attachment or is so situated that all-round bearings cannot be taken, the difficulty can be got over by using a PELORUS. This instrument is simply an adjustable compass card, called a dumb-card, pivoted on a gimballed base or frame fitted with a lubber's line and a rotatable sighting attachment. The pelorus is firmly fixed on the cabin top, or in some other position where a good all-round view is obtainable, with its lubber line correctly in the fore-and-aft direction. Each time a bearing is required, clamp the dumb-card in the position in which its lubber's line reads the compass course steered. A bearing taken by the sighting attachment and read off on the dumb-card will then be the same as though it were taken from the compass itself.

Heeling Error. The little sailing ship is sometimes troubled by the deviation of the compass changing with the angle of heel. This is HEELING ERROR, and is due to the action of ironwork below (or, rarely with little ships, above) the level of the compass magnet system. It does not often amount to much, but since it is obviously impracticable to construct and use a deviation table for angles of heel as well as directions of ship's head, the compass-adjuster should be called in to get rid of any appreciable heeling error found to be present. Fig. 28 shows the heeling effect action.

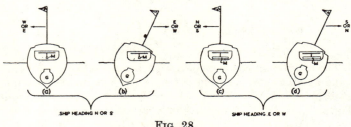

FIG. 28.

In Fig. 28 an engine G is installed below the compass which is represented for simplicity as having a single bar magnet M. If the ship is heading N or S by compass, as in (a) and (b), the magnet M lies fore-and-aft, and the result of heeling the ship from (a) to (b) is to move the engine laterally relative to the magnet and, therefore, to change the deviation. If the ship is heading E or W, as in (c) and (d), the length of the magnet is athwartship, and the result of heel is, therefore, to move the engine along the length of the magnet M, producing practically no effect on the deviation. *Therefore, heeling error is a maximum when heading N or S and practically zero when heading E or W.* Accordingly, heeling error may be tested for by heading the ship N or S by compass, with the sheet free, observing a couple of marks in line so that she can be kept heading in the same direction without the compass, and then heeling her well over by hauling the sheet in. If the compass reading changes materially, there is heeling error and the adjuster should be called in.

Checking the Compass. The factors causing deviation are liable to change with time, especially in the case of a steel ship headed in one direction for a long period. This, of course, occurs during laying up, and therefore the ship should be swung for deviation at least at the beginning of each season. *Thereafter lose no opportunity of checking the compass when on passage.* Check it when passing a couple of objects in line and marked on the chart so that their bearing is known, or when passing up a narrow channel in a direction given by the chart; and, generally, whenever opportunity arises.

Caution. In a little ship with an auxiliary engine, the deviation may not be the same when the engine is running and when it is off. Check this, and if necessary have two deviation tables, one for each condition. Beware of badly installed electric lighting wires for the compass. An electrified wire produces magnetism, but if the " go " and " return " lighting wires are close side by side their effects should cancel out. Test by switching the light on and off on different courses. *Beware of all movable ironwork.* Moving iron ballast to alter trim, shifting spare chain about, storing petrol-cans in cockpit lockers near the compass, changing over iron cylinders of cooking and lighting gas, are all typical causes of changes in deviation which are sometimes unsuspected. In short be suspicious of anything movable of iron or steel near the compass, *and regard compass checking as a regular precaution.*

CHAPTER VIII

NAVIGATIONAL INSTRUMENTS: THE SEXTANT

Advantages of the Sextant for Coastal Navigation. There are innumerable occasions, not only in celestial navigation by the heavenly bodies but also in coastal navigation by shore marks, when much invaluable assistance can be obtained by measuring angles, and the sextant is the instrument mainly used at sea for this purpose. In many little ships the sextant is apt to be regarded as useful only for deep-water navigation and is entirely neglected for coastal work. It admittedly requires much more practice to use with confidence than the compass and the occasions when it can be employed coastwise are less numerous, but when those occasions do arise it usually gives results which are substantially more accurate and reliable. In practice a little ship can seldom be steered on a really steady course except in the kindest of weathers, so that a compass card is more or less continuously swinging to and fro to some extent. Bearing errors, which are sometimes quite large and frequently unsuspected, can creep in from this cause, which is not present with the sextant. Personal errors of observation, again commonly unsuspected, are generally considerably larger with the compass than with the sextant. In general, the navigator who is accustomed to the use of the sextant knows, when he has taken an observation with the instrument, whether it is reliable or not. It is either a good observation or it is *obviously* a bad one—and that is often more than can be said for compass bearings taken in a seaway when the ship is bobbing about even moderately. *The embryo navigator is strongly recommended to practise with the sextant, at first in good weather conditions, as often as possible.* It is like riding a bicycle: at first it will seem an impossible accomplishment and then, suddenly, you find you have got the trick and can do it.

Principle of the Sextant. The sextant (see Fig. 29 (a)) consists essentially of a strong rigid frame carrying a fixed mirror F, called the HORIZON MIRROR, and a telescope D, which is often interchangeable. Near the top of the frame is pivoted an arm C, called the INDEX, on which is fixed another mirror M, termed the INDEX MIRROR. The bottom A of the frame, known as the ARC, is circularly curved, with the pivot of the index as centre, so that as the index is swung over the arc, the angle between the two mirrors is changed. On the arc is engraved

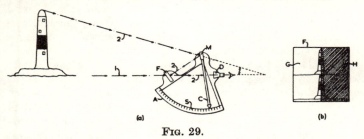

(a)   (b)

FIG. 29.

a scale S, against which the position of the index can be read. When the two mirrors M and F are parallel, the scale reading (if there is no index error) is 0. The index mirror M is an ordinary very high quality mirror, but the horizon mirror F, shown in face view in Fig. 29 (b), is only half silvered at H over the half nearer the frame, the other half G being of plain glass. Light can reach the eye of an observer at the telescope by two paths, namely, the path 1 directly through the clear glass G, and the zig-zag path 2 by reflection via the silvered surfaces at M and F. Accordingly two images can be seen simultaneously, and when the mirrors M and F are exactly parallel these two images exactly superimpose and appear as one. By moving the index, and thereby putting the mirror M at an angle to the mirror F, the two images can be made to separate and one point in one image can be brought over a different point in the other. In Fig. 29 the index has been adjusted to bring the top of the lighthouse, in the reflected image, on to the sea surface in the direct image. The scale S is so marked that when two different points in the images are thus brought on to one another, the scale reads the angle Z, shown by the dotted lines, subtended at the observer between the straight lines from those points to the observer. In Fig. 29 (a) therefore, the scale reading is the angle Z, at the observer, between the top of the lighthouse and the sea surface.

Modern Sextant Construction. A typical example of good modern sextant construction is illustrated in Plate IV. This sextant is of the micrometer endless tangent screw type, which is so much more convenient to use and easy to read than the more old-fashioned vernier type that the latter is becoming obsolescent for little ship use and will accordingly not be described here. The micrometer arrangement is separately shown in Plate V. The index C carries at its lower end a rotatable drum-like head B, which reads against a fixed vernier scale E, and drives a shaft J on which is an endless screw (not shown) engaging teeth cut on the back of the arc. Thus, by rotating the head B, the index can be moved very accurately over the arc A for fine adjustment. By pressing the button K, the endless screw can be brought out of mesh with the teeth and the index moved quickly for coarse adjustment. Degrees are read directly by the arrow L against the scale S, and minutes are read directly by the arrow N against the scale on the head B. The vernier scale E (some very good modern sextants do not have one) has six markings which occupy exactly the same distance as five of the minute markings on the head B. Accordingly, if the head B is rotated from the position shown in Plate V, to bring the 1' line on B opposite the first mark below the arrow N on E, it will have been moved through a distance corresponding to 1/6th of a minute, i.e. 10″; if the second minute mark is brought opposite the second mark below the arrow on E the vernier reading is 20″; if the third minute mark is brought opposite the third vernier mark the reading is 30″, and so on. Thus, degrees are read directly by L, minutes directly by B, and 10-second portions of a minute by the vernier E. Glass shades P of different densities can be swung in front of the index and horizon mirrors M and F to adjust the light reaching the eye by the two different paths, and there is a small electric lamp Q (a convenient extra, this, for night work) for illuminating the scales. The scale S on the arc A extends in one direction from 0 to about 130° and, back from 0, for about 5°. This back part of the scale is called the EXCESS OF ARC, and readings taken on it are called OFF THE ARC as distinct from readings taken forward of zero, which are called ON THE ARC.

Testing a Sextant. It is wise to know enough about the sextant to be able to test your own from time to time to see that it has not been damaged, or to make an intelligent, second-hand purchase. Second-hand sextants which are not heavy enough for a kedge anchor and no good for anything else are by no means uncommon. The main faults to look for are:

1. Worn or damaged pivot. To test for this remove such parts carrying the telescope as are necessary to enable the index to come right off the arc, then take hold of the index arm at the far end and *gently* try it for shake in its pivot. A trifle of shake is permissible. See that the index swings freely and smoothly. A binding pivot is usually much more serious than one that is a trifle loose.

2. Bent frame (a usually fatal fault). Hold the sextant horizontally, arc away from you, and look obliquely into the index mirror so that you can see the arc and its reflection as at A and A′ in Plate VI. Then move the index round the arc, following the arc and its reflection with the eye. If the space between the reflected and actual arcs changes, the frame is probably bent; anyway, the pivot is not properly at right angles to it.

3. " Dud " mirrors. If the mirrors have no obvious blemish, look obliquely into each in turn at the reflection of some object and move the sextant about. The reflection should remain clearly outlined and undistorted. Mirrors are not very expensive and this fault is usually fairly easily rectified.

4. Backlash in the micrometer. Measure an angle by taking a sight on some fairly distant object, *e.g.* bring a roof-top down to the top of a lamp-post. Do this by

rotating the micrometer head always in the same direction. When you have read the angle rotate the drum further in the same direction and then measure the angle again by rotating the drum back in the opposite direction. The two measurements should be the same. Backlash can usually be cured by adjustment.

5. Collimation error (telescope not parallel to plane of arc). Set the sextant down horizontally on its legs and sight across the frame at a distant roof-top. Then, without moving the instrument, look through the telescope, keeping the eye in line with the telescope axis. The roof-top should appear across the middle of the field of view. It is uncommon to find this fault *alone* in a reasonably modern sextant.

Sextant Adjustments. There are three main adjustments of the sextant, all made by means of screws at the backs of the two mirrors. They are: (1) adjusting the index mirror perpendicular to the plane of the instrument; (2) adjusting the horizon mirror perpendicular to the plane of the instrument; (3) adjusting the horizon mirror parallel to the index mirror when the sextant reads zero. The adjustments should be made when necessary, *and only when necessary*, in the order in which they have been mentioned. The first eliminates " error of perpendicularity," the second eliminates " side error," and the third eliminates " index error."

1. First adjustment: Index mirror. Hold the sextant horizontally, as in Plate VI, with the eye close to the index mirror and the index at about the middle of the arc. The actual arc A (see Plate VI) and the reflected arc A' should appear in one line. If they are not, the screw R (Plate IV) at the back of the index mirror requires adjustment.

2. Second adjustment: Horizon mirror for side error. Hold the sextant vertically, as in ordinary use, and with the index near zero look through the telescope at a star of low altitude. Operate the micrometer to make the reflected and direct images move over one another. They should move exactly over each other, appearing as one when they pass. If they pass side by side, the screw T (Plate IV),

furthest away from the frame at the back of the horizon mirror, needs adjustment.

3. Third adjustment: Horizon mirror for index error. Set the index exactly at zero and, holding the sextant vertically in the ordinary way, look through the telescope at a clear horizon by day or, better still, at a star by night. If there is no index error the direct and reflected horizons will appear as one unbroken line or the star as one image. If the horizon appears with a break in it or the star gives two images, one above the other, adjust the micrometer until the break disappears or the two images merge into one. The sextant reading then obtained is the INDEX ERROR, which is + if the reading is off the arc, — if the reading is on the arc. If the error is small, not more than 3′ to 4′ make no adjustment but simply log it for future use, adding a plus error to subsequent readings and subtracting a minus one. If the error is larger, the screw U (Plate IV), nearer the frame at the back of the horizon mirror, needs adjustment. *Make a practice of checking the index error frequently; it takes only a minute to do.* You may find that each of these adjustments slightly upsets the previous ones, which may accordingly require a little re-adjustment.

Caution. *Never make unnecessary adjustments* and avoid repeated " monkeying " to get rid of trifling errors. In particular, do not try to maintain zero index error. A small index error, if you know how much it is, does no harm at all. Every time you adjust the screws you loosen them slightly, and loose screws may introduce varying errors which are larger than those you are trying to correct.

Choice of a Sextant. Telescopes and Extras. The standard size of sextant, with an arc of 6 to 7 inches radius, is, in the author's opinion, best for little ship work, though nowadays quite satisfactory smaller sextants are made. An index mirror of large size is a material advantage, and may make all the difference to use in a seaway. A multiplicity of telescopes— inverting telescopes and so on—are unnecessary in the little ship. The so-called star telescope, such as that shown at D in Plate IV—a short telescope with a large object glass—

is all that is required, and may be kept permanently shipped (if the sextant case will allow of it) and used for all purposes. Most of the "special" (and expensive) extras, such as artificial bubble horizon attachments and so on, are not intended for little ship use and quite unsuited thereto. The name of a good maker is worth having on a sextant—perhaps more so if buying second-hand.

Use and Care of the Sextant. Always hold the sextant by the handle, not by the frame. If it is necessary to lift it by the frame to take it out of the case, lift it centrally—never by one corner. Keep it in its case until you want it and then put it back at once—*do not put it down loose in the cockpit or cabin.* When replacing it in its case do not forget to turn any clamps fitted to prevent its banging about inside, and stow the case, if possible, flat and with the lid uppermost. Keep a piece of clean chamois leather (not cloth) in the case, and *lightly* wipe over the glasses to dry them after use. *Never apply force to the mirrors*, either when drying them or otherwise. Occasionally, and sparingly, lubricate the moving parts and wipe over the rubbing surfaces of the arc with an oiled leather. The thin oil containing graphite and sold to add to the lubricating oil of motor cars when " running in " is excellent for this purpose. Accustom yourself to holding the sextant vertically. This can be practised by bringing the sun down to the horizon and then, with your eye at the telescope, rocking the sextant about the centre line of the telescope as axis. Movement away from the vertical will then bring the sun out of contact with the horizon, so that the vertical can easily be found this way. Find a good firm position to stand in when using the instrument; in most little ships the best position is to brace yourself with your back against the mast, though sometimes the forward end of the cockpit is quite good. In a seaway take your observation approximately, then wait for a " smooth," or until you are on the top of a wave, and finish the observation. If necessary, heave-to for a moment or two. The sextant, for all its accuracy, is a robust instrument: properly cared for, it will last a life-time; manhandled it may not last one season.

PLATE II

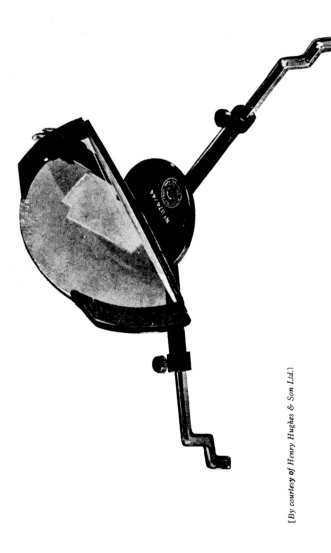

[By courtesy of Henry Hughes & Son Ltd.]

ADJUSTABLE TRIPOD LEG COMPASS MAGNIFIER

PLATE VII

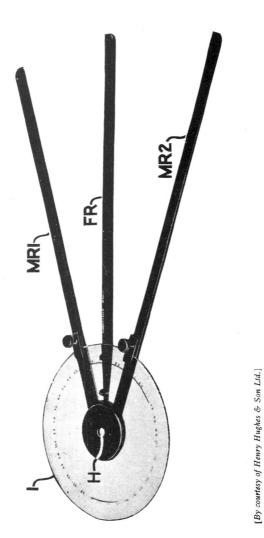

SIMPLE VERNIER-LESS STATION POINTER

Plastic Sextants. Metal sextants, like that shown in Plate IV for example, are costly instruments, but plastic sextants, costing about the same as a hand bearing compass—often less— are now available. The Author does not consider them good enough for Astro-Navigation, though some of the big shipping companies use them for the training of apprentices in taking sights, but they are quite adequate for coastal navigation. However, a certain amount of special precaution should be taken in their use. One of their main defects is that, being made of plastic material, they do not hold their adjustments anything like as well as metal sextants do and, in particular, they show a marked tendency to change in index error, especially after exposure to sunlight. This causes no difficulties with horizontal sextant angles, for which observations to an accuracy of 1° is all that is ever required in coastal navigation practice, but it can cause possibly serious errors with vertical sextant angles, for which readings which are correct to a minute of arc may be necessary. *Therefore, every time you use a plastic sextant for a vertical angle, check it for index error—it may well be substantially different from what it was last time the instrument was used—and never leave a plastic sextant lying exposed to sunlight.* (Horizontal and vertical sextant angles are dealt with in Chapter XIII).

CHAPTER IX

NAVIGATIONAL INSTRUMENTS: THE LOG AND LEAD

The Patent Log. The distance a ship moves endwise through the water is measured by the PATENT LOG, which is really a marine mileometer and works in a generally similar way. The taffrail type of log is the most suitable for little ship work. It consists of a rotator 1, which is towed astern by a length of plaited log line 2 the inboard end of which hooks on to the shaft 3 of a weighted wheel 4, called the governor,

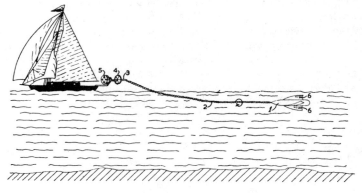

FIG. 30.

which drives the register 5 removably fixed to a bracket on the quarter so that the line and rotator are clear of the wake. The rotator has curved fins 6, so that as it is towed along, it rotates at a speed proportional to the speed at which it is pulled through the water. This rotation is transmitted through the log line to the governor, which acts as a flywheel, and thus drives the register, which is merely a case containing a train of gears driving pointers indicating, as a rule, tens of miles, miles, and tenths of a mile. The pointers can be set to zero by opening the face of the register.

Care of the Log. The accuracy of the log depends on the rotator, and especially its fins, being undamaged ; the log line being of the right length for your ship (too long a line makes the log read high—too short a line makes it read low); and the register running freely. The rotator is robust and not easily damaged, so the first requirement can be satisfied by ordinary care. Keep it in its box when out of use, and dry it and rub it over with oil before putting it away. Remember to " hand " the log (*i.e.* take it in) when entering shallows, otherwise it may bump along the bottom and will certainly do so if the ship loses speed ; remember to hand the log before going astern under power, otherwise the log line and propeller will make an acquaintance that may ripen into fast friendship ; and be careful not to bang the rotator against the hull when taking it inboard. As regards the length of line, follow the maker's instructions on this point (they will always advise you if you tell them the approximate size, speed and type of your ship), until the line has stretched and settled down. Then check the log as described below. *It is wise always to start a new line too long.* Remember to lubricate the register at the proper intervals in accordance with maker's instructions.

Checking the Log. The easiest way to do this is to sail in company with a chummy ship whose log is known to be correct, or has a known error, and compare log readings. Alternatively take two runs (preferably under power and at the same engine speed) in opposite directions over a measured distance—the numerous measured miles are admirable for this purpose—carefully reading the log for each run and carefully timing each run to the nearest second. Work out the actual mean speed for the two runs by dividing the measured distance by each of the two times and finding the mean. Then work out the mean speed by log, by dividing the total distance recorded by the total time. A comparison of the two mean speeds gives the log error.

Example. In two successive runs in opposite directions over a measured mile, the log distances are ·9 mile and 1·4 miles and the times taken are exactly 10 minutes and 15 minutes respectively. What was the log error?

$$\text{Actual speed one way} \quad = \quad \frac{1 \times 60}{10} \quad = \quad 6 \text{ knots}$$

$$\text{Actual speed back} \quad = \quad \frac{1 \times 60}{15} \quad = \quad 4 \text{ knots}$$

$$\text{Actual average speed} \quad = \quad \frac{6+4}{2} \quad = \quad 5 \text{ knots}$$

Average speed by log (·9+1·4 miles in 10+15 minutes)

$$= \quad \frac{2·3 \times 60}{25} \quad = \quad 5·52 \text{ knots}$$

Log reads high by 5·52−5   =   0·52 in 5·52

$$\therefore \text{ per cent. error} \quad = \quad \frac{·52 \times 100}{5·52} \quad = \quad \text{(nearly enough) 9\%.}$$

A log check of this kind should be carried out on a calm day and the log should be streamed and allowed to settle down at the test speed before actually entering the measured distance. The two runs in opposite directions are for the purpose of cancelling out the effects of any tidal stream, and for a similar reason the check is best done in the first *or* in the last hour of the stream.

If the log error is not more than 10 per cent. it is not worth while adjusting the line. Thus, in the above example the error should be merely noted and allowed for by multiplying any subsequent distance, measured by the log, by $\frac{100}{109}$.

Chance Errors of the Log. The log will tend to read a little low in a strong following sea. It will also read low—seriously low—if anything fouls the line or rotator. Therefore give an eye occasionally to the governor to see that it is running regularly, and haul up and inspect the line every now and then if there is any risk of picking up weed. *If you are towing a dinghy see that it is clear of the log line*.

Streaming and Handing the Log. When streaming a log,

hook the line on to the governor first and then pass the rotator gently astern so that the line does not take up with a jerk at the end. Stream it some minutes before it is wanted to give it time to settle down, and then, when you have reached your " departure," *i.e.* the point from which you intend to record distance, set the pointers to zero. When handing the log, haul in a few feet of line, unhook from the governor, and continue to haul in over one quarter while paying out the hook end over the other. Finally, when the rotator is aboard, haul the line in again. This will prevent the line being twisted into snarls due to the action of the rotator while hauling in.

Caution. Log and Distance made Good. The distance recorded by a log is only the distance travelled by the ship forward through the water, relative to the water. *This is not the same as the distance travelled over the ground,* which is the DISTANCE MADE GOOD. The log does *not* record (1) distance moved over the ground due to a tidal or other stream, or (2) distance moved over the ground due to the ship being blown sideways through the water, *i.e.* LEEWAY. Distances moved forward through the water *at very low speeds,* for example when a ship is hove to or " ghosting " in very light airs, may either not be recorded at all or recorded at less than their true values.

Rough-and-Ready Approximation. In the absence of a proper log a rough-and-ready estimate of the distance travelled through the water may be made by estimating the speed at intervals and multiplying the average speed by the time sailed. The speed may be approximately estimated by throwing a piece of driftwood well ahead of the ship and then sailing past it, observing with the second hand of a watch, how long it takes for two marks, a known distance apart on deck, to pass. The two marks should, of course, be as far apart in the fore-and-aft direction as possible. The speed calculation becomes a matter of very simple arithmetic if it is remembered that 1 knot=(very nearly) 100 ft. per minute.

Example. A ship, in sailing past a piece of driftwood, takes $3\frac{1}{2}$ seconds between the time her forward chain plate is abreast of it and the time her jib sheet cleat in the cockpit is abreast of it. The distance between these two points is 28 feet. What was the speed?

28 ft. in $3\frac{1}{2}$ seconds $=\dfrac{28 \times 60}{3\frac{1}{2}}$ feet per minute$=480$ ft./min.

$$\text{Speed} \quad = \quad 4\cdot8 \text{ knots.}$$

The Lead. In these days echo sounders are, understandably, much more used than the LEAD and, indeed, generally give considerably greater accuracy—it requires more skill than is commonly supposed to get a reliable sounding with a lead—but they do sometimes cease to function. A lead and line should therefore always be carried as a standby. A lead of about 10 lbs weight on a line of about 30 fathoms (approximately 3 ft. more than 54 metres) is convenient for little ship work. It should have a hollow in the base which can be filled with tallow to enable a sample of the sea bottom to be brought up, if required, for comparison with the chart. This is called ARMING THE LEAD, and is sometimes useful in helping to find your position, since the nature of the sea bottom at different places is given on the chart. A second lead, of about half the weight of the first, on a line of about half the length, is a handy accessory for inshore work. It is also a good tip to mark out a long boat-hook, spinnaker boom, or other spar which is carried anyway, with numbered, brightly painted rings at suitable close intervals, *e.g.* one foot apart. Such a "sounding spar" is invaluable on many occasion, for example, when beating up a shallow river. The traditional markings of the hand lead are not well suited for little ship use and many amateurs prefer to invent their own. The following marks, inserted at the distances stated along the line, are suggested as convenient for little ships. They have been so calculated that the same marks will serve for use with both fathom and metric charts and, although none of them is precisely correctly positioned, the errors in practical use are entirely negligible, being only a matter of inches up to 17 fathoms, and only 1 ft. at 20 fathoms:—

Distance along line		Marks	Sounding	
			fathoms	metres
6'	4"	1 knot	1	2
12'	6"	2 knots	2	4
29'	8"	1 leather strip	5	9
42'	4"	2 leather strips	7	13
59'	6"	3 leather strips	10	18
78'	4"	1 parrel line ball	13	24
89'	4"	2 leather strips	15	27
101'	10"	3 leather strips	17	31
119'	0"	2 parrel line balls	20	36

Caution. A cast of the lead will be accurate only if the line is straight up and down when read. The faster the ship is going through the water, the more difficult it is to secure this result. If necessary, heave to or ease away the sheets to take a cast. *Any error will be an error on the dangerous side* —it will tell you that the water is deeper than in fact it is. *Never rely on a single cast if the matter is of importance:* always take two or three. Remember that the depth given by a cast is not the depth as shown on the chart: it is the chart depth plus the height of the tide at the time.

CHAPTER X

PLANNING THE PASSAGE: LEEWAY. CURRENT TRIANGLES

The importance of adequately planning a projected passage in advance cannot be over-emphasised, and the smaller the little ship, the more the need for preliminary chart work. What is easy and quick to do in the quiet of harbour is apt to be far more difficult at sea, and human weakness being what it is, a navigator working in an ill-lit cabin in bad weather conditions will commit blunders that would never occur under better conditions. Many a little ship has been lost or damaged due to such errors.

Selecting the Track to be made Good. The first thing to decide is, obviously, the track to be made good. Draw a straight line lightly in pencil on the chart between the beginning and end of the projected passage. Then carefully examine the chart along the line, and for a fair distance on both sides of it, for any dangers to navigation—sandbanks, shallows, rocks, races, and so on. If the straight-line track is clear of such dangers, all well and good: it is clearly the track to follow if you can. The straight line may, however, cross sandbanks or other impassable obstructions, in which case a series of lines avoiding the obstructions must be chosen. Sometimes the straight line, though itself passing over sufficient water everywhere, may run so close to dangers that a small error in navigation will involve running the ship aground. In such a case, examine the chart for reliable navigation aids by which an accurate position can be obtained *before* getting too near the dangers. Prominent, *recognisable* shore marks and lightships are reliable navigation aids for this purpose; buoys are not. Although lighted main channel buoys round our coasts are seldom out of position, their range of visibility from a little ship is quite small, especially by daylight, and on those very common days when visibility is markedly different in different directions, a buoy only a mile away, *e.g.* up sun, may be very difficult to spot when another buoy, two or three times as far away, down sun, is plainly visible.

With a power ship, the chosen tracks can be followed fairly closely, but when under sail adverse winds may compel considerable departures from the lines on the chart. Accordingly, while a track which threads its way among adjacent sandbanks might be the best for a power craft, it might involve hazardous navigation under sail; and a track which would be satisfactory under sail with a commanding free wind might well be very much the opposite with a foul wind.

Where the chart gives you a choice of tracks for the same passage, remember the effect of tidal streams; they may mean that the shortest route is not the quickest. Also, in making your choice, have regard to the different degrees of protection afforded over the different possible routes in the prevailing weather conditions: a track inside sandbanks to windward might experience so much less sea than the one outside as to be actually faster, not to mention more comfortable, despite being longer than the outside track.

In selecting tracks, remember the effect of tide upon the depths as shown by the chart. Work out in advance the approximate times you will be at different places in the passage, and note not only the extra depths the tide will give you at those places, *but also whether those depths will be increasing or decreasing when you reach them*. If you " touch " on a falling tide you may be aground a long time, so do not select a track that involves tricky and close navigation on a falling tide if there is a good alternative. For the same reason *never, if you can help it, navigate to the limits of the depths at high water*. If, for example, a high water height is 10 ft., navigate as though it were only 7, thus giving yourself half-a-fathom " for luck " : you may need it !

Timing the Start of a Passage. The factors governing choice of the best time to start a passage are inter-connected with those governing choice of the tracks to be followed. The main considerations are usually wind, tides, and tidal streams. Clearly, full advantage should be taken of any favourable stream, and though obviously no general rule can be laid down in a matter of this kind, it commonly pays to start a coastal passage on the last of a foul tidal stream, when it is weak, in order to obtain the whole benefit of a following fair stream. Sometimes the state of tide or of tidal stream at some point in the passage or at the end of the passage is the determining factor in choosing the best starting time. For example, if making Chichester with any risk of strong winds between about SE and SW, such an ugly sea gets up over and near the bar when the water is shallow, especially on the ebb, that it is wise to time your arrival at the bar near high water, with the flood stream still running in. Again, if bound from the Channel into the North Sea, or vice versa, much can be gained by timing yourself to arrive where the tides divide in the Dungeness–Dover area so as to reach there on the last of the flood stream on one side, and carry on into the beginning of the ebb on the other.

Examples of the practical application of some of these considerations are given with reference to Fig. 31, which is a highly simplified and rough sketch of the Thames Estuary. Suppose a sailing ship, with a speed of about 5 knots when sailing free, is bound from Harwich to Ramsgate. An examination of the Atlas of Tidal Streams for the Thames Estuary shows that the streams are setting into the estuary until about an hour before H.W. Sheerness. Accordingly, with the wind anywhere in the northern half of the circle, by leaving Harwich at about 6 hours after H.W. Sheerness, there would be a fair stream enabling the ship easily to reach a point off the NE end of the Gunfleet at about 4 hours before H.W. Sheerness, at which time the stream is setting strongly SW into the East Swin and Barrow Deep. In these circumstances, the further 15 miles or so to the Mid-Barrow LV could easily be covered by about 1 hour before H.W. Sheerness. The course would then be changed for the Edinburgh LV, so that the ship would probably be well on in the Edinburgh Channel, and even approaching the Tongue Tower, before any very strong foul stream was encountered. This track, shown in broken lines, is pre-eminently safe, being in well-buoyed main channels all the way, with plenty of good marks for

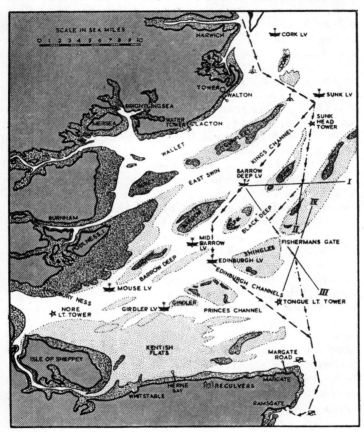

Fig. 31.

position finding. In short, a " no-worry " passage. *With visibility and other conditions good*, however, a considerable saving could be made by modifying the track as shown in chain lines, going to the Sunk Head Tower and then down the Black Deep, cutting across Fisherman's Gate to pass the Tongue Tower on the east side. This track is much more tricky. It involves crossing at an angle into the Black Deep with a strong tidal stream well on the port beam, and then passing through the narrow Fisherman's Gate, again with cross streams. In thickish weather, therefore, or with a foul wind or a wind so light that the narrow Gate would not be reached until the tide was beginning to fall again, this short-cut passage would be an unwise choice. So long, however, as conditions were good and the visibility allowed the main channel buoys to be picked up at a reasonable distance and the light vessels and towers to be seen clearly at 7 or 8 miles or so, it would be safe enough. For such a passage the pre-liminary chart work should include drawing on the chart compass bearings, by which the turning points on the track could be checked: for example, the bearing line I from the Barrow Deep LV, crossing the back bearing II on the Sunk Head Tower, would "fix" the turn into the Black Deep; the bearing line III from the Barrow Deep LV would help in leading through Fisherman's Gate ; and the bearing line IV from the Tongue Tower would safeguard you against turning to starboard too soon in the Gate. Such bearings as these, drawn lightly on the chart, and with their compass readings, *corrected in advance for variation and (if the ship's compass is to be used) deviation*, written on the ends of the lines (where the legends I, II, III, and IV are written), would be of great assistance. Again, ring round in advance any lettered or numbered tidal stream positions on or near the track, and mark the tidal stream "panel" on the chart as already described in Chapter I with reference to Fig. 5. *In short, anticipate, so far as you can, any navigational information you are likely to want at sea by doing necessary chart work in harbour.*

Timing a Passage. It is a wise precaution to work out in advance the estimated times of arrival at major recognisable points in a passage. There are many things which may go wrong in little ship navigation and not be observed until long after they happen. For example, a tired or inexperienced helmsman may steer a wrong course for half his watch, or the log may become fouled or damaged unobserved. With a quadrantal compass it is quite easy for a helmsman to let his attention wander for a short time and then to pick up a wrong course having the same numbered degree marking as the correct course, so that at some unknown time in his watch he unconsciously changes a correct course of say, N 10° E to a wrong one of N 10° W. In such circumstances the ship's dead-reckoning position, and perhaps her track also, will become increasingly in error from the moment the trouble occurs. If the navigator has prepared in advance an estimated time-table giving the times and directions at which important recognisable marks, such as major lights, should be seen, he will have at hand a ready means of checking his navigation and receiving warning if anything has gone wrong. On a night passage it is a good plan to leave with the helmsmen taking the watches a list of the lights which should be observed during the night, with the times and directions in which they should appear, instructions being given to call the navigator if any of them does not show up reasonably near the proper time and direction.

Deliberate Error. When a passage is expected to terminate in daylight at a port on a coast, such as the Dutch coast, which is not rich in conspicuous marks, it is frequently of advantage to set course to make a landfall a few miles to one side of the port, instead of aiming at the port itself. This practice, which is termed introducing a DELIBERATE or KNOWN ERROR, has the obvious advantage that, on sighting the coast, the navigator will know which way to turn to reach his destination, even if he does not recognise the part of the coast first seen. Had he steered directly for his destination and, due to some unknown error, failed to find it in view on sighting land, he might well be in doubt as to whether it lay to port or starboard. Moreover, even if he recognised the coast, he might find himself down tide or down wind, or both, of his destination. The navigator under power should, other considerations permitting, shape his course to make a landfall up-tide of his final port; under sail, both wind and stream must be considered and the landfall selected to ensure the easiest passage along the coast to port.

Leeway. A course steered and a course made good will seldom be the same. The movements of a ship with reference to the sea bottom comprise three factors : (1) movement of the ship *endwise* through the water; (2) movement of the ship *sideways* through the water; and (3) movement of the water itself. The first of these movements is the result of the course steered; the second is LEEWAY; and the third is due to the tidal stream. Any or all of these three factors may be present. They occur simultaneously, but it is convenient, for explanatory purposes to consider them separately. Consider a model boat Y (Fig. 32a) steered N at 1 knot across a tank W of water. Then, so long as this is all that is happening, the movement of the boat in relation to the floor F, on which the tank stands, is the same as the movement through the water. In other words the COURSE AND DISTANCE RUN (*i.e.* the distance as it would be measured by a log L towed behind the boat) are the same as the COURSE AND DISTANCE MADE GOOD over the floor F. Now suppose that (Fig. 32b) while steering N at 1 knot, the boat is subjected to a side wind which blows it laterally eastwards through the water at half a knot. The course steered is the same as in Fig. 32a, but the real movement through the water is along the chain line X. The angle between the line X and the course steered, *i.e.* the fore-and-aft line of the boat, is the LEEWAY ANGLE. It will be observed that, since the boat is moving sideways as well as endwise through the water, this leeway angle will exist between the direction in which the log line streams out aft and the fore-and-aft direction. Similarly the wake, if any, will make the same angle with the fore-and-aft line.

Measurement of and Allowance for Leeway. Since leeway can be seen from the wake or log line, it can readily be judged by eye, or measured and allowed for, by applying to the course steered a correction angle equal to the leeway angle. To measure leeway, take a bearing along the wake or the log line (the former is usually easier in practice) and compare it with the course reversed. The difference, if any, is the leeway.

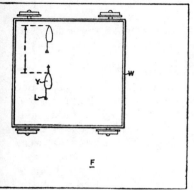

FIG. 32a.

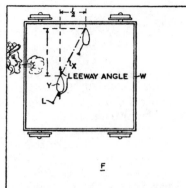

FIG. 32b.

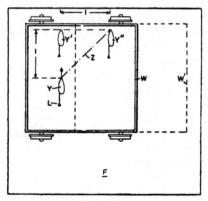

FIG. 32c.

If the bearing is taken along the log line, be careful to take it from a point as nearly as possible over the inboard end of the line and in the direction of the log line.

   Example.   When steering N 10° E, full and by on the port tack, the direction of the wake is observed to be S 15° W.

What is the course, corrected to allow for leeway?

Course steered, N 10° E.   Reversed, S 10° W.

Bearing of wake, S 15° W.

Leeway, $\overline{5°}$

∴ Course actually followed through the water is 5° to lee of the steered course, *i.e.* (since the wind is on the port side) N 15° E.

In general, a modern yacht under plain sail, full and by, 50° off the wind, will have a leeway angle of about 5°. If under plain sail the angle is more than this, you are sailing too close.

Tidal Stream Drift. Now consider the effect of a tidal stream. Referring once more to the model boat and tank, the effect is as though the whole tank W, boat and all, were moved bodily over the floor F while the boat is moving across the tank. In Fig. 32c suppose that, while the boat is steering N at 1 knot across the tank W, the latter is being wheeled bodily eastwards across the floor at 1 knot. The movement of the boat in relation to the water is exactly as in Fig. 32a, but the movement in relation to the floor F, *i.e.* the course and distance made good, is along the chain line Z. It is obviously the resultant of the boat movement and the tank movement. If, while the boat is moving from Y to Y' across the tank, the latter is moved from the position shown in full lines at W to the position shown in dotted lines at W', the final position of the boat will be at Y''. The line Z, followed by the boat, is the third and longest side of a triangle of which one side represents in direction and length the boat movement, and the second represents in direction and length the tank (tidal stream) movement. Note that the log line and wake are in the fore-and-aft line of the ship, for the latter moves with the stream and is, in effect, part of it. *You cannot see a tidal stream by looking at the water unless you have some object, fixed to the ground, to judge it by, for your ship moves with it.*

Current Triangle. To allow for the effect of a tidal stream, simply construct to scale (any convenient scale) a triangle like that of Fig. 33. Suppose a ship is steered to move through the water in a true direction (corrected for leeway, if any) of 045°, her speed being 5 knots. Suppose she is in a tidal stream setting 135° at 2 knots. Draw, to any scale, a line A–B, in direction 045°, whose length represents 5 knots. From B draw, to the same scale, a line B–C in direction 135°, whose length represents 2 knots. The point B is where the ship would have reached if there were no stream. The point C is where she will reach owing to the stream. The line A–C

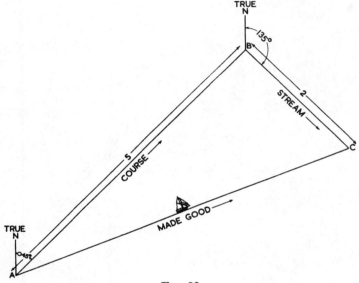

FIG. 33.

represents, in direction, the course made good, and the length of this line represents the speed over the ground, *i.e.* the real speed. Fig. 33 is an example of a CURRENT TRIANGLE. Whenever the effect of a cross stream is required to be ascertained or (more commonly) it is required to find out what course to steer to cancel out such an effect, a current triangle is constructed. It can be made to any scale *so long as the same scale is used for all its sides.*

Course to Steer in a Stream. Fig. 33 illustrates the case where the course steered and the tidal stream are known, and

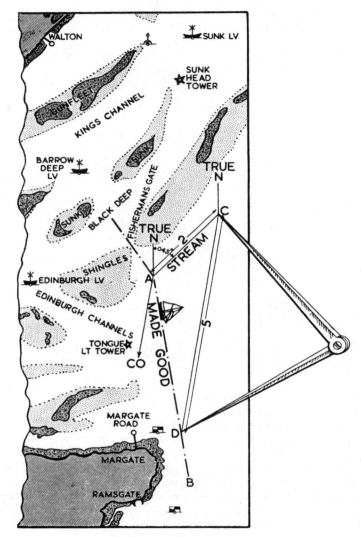

Fig. 34.

the triangle is constructed to discover the track made good. More usually, however, the problem presents itself rather differently to the navigator : he wants to know what course to steer so as to make good an already chosen track despite the effect of a known tidal stream. Suppose a ship, sailing at 5 knots, has passed through Fisherman's Gate (Fig. 34) to point A and desires to make good the track A–B to the North Foreland. Suppose the stream is setting 045°/2 knots. If the ship simply drifted with the stream, she would travel in one hour 2 miles in the direction 045° to a point C. Draw the line A–C in the direction 045° and of a length to represent, to any convenient scale, 2 miles. Then open the dividers to represent the ship's travel of 5 miles (to the same scale), and with one point at C, observe where the other point cuts the line A–B at D. Then C–D is parallel to the direction (CO) in which the ship must be headed to make good a track along A–B, and the speed made good along this track will be the length of A–D on whatever scale has been used for A–C and C–D. In the case illustrated the speed made good along A–B is about $3\frac{1}{2}$ knots.

Varying Streams. Where a stream varies hour by hour, the same method may be extended to enable a single figure to be drawn for several hours. Thus, referring to Fig. 35, suppose that in the first hour the stream sets 045°/2 knots; in the second hour it sets 090°/2 knots; and in the third hour 135°/1 knot. As before, find where the ship would get to if she merely drifted, and then find the course from there. In the first hour she would drift to C_1; in the first two hours to C_2; and in the three hours to C_3. It does not in the least matter if these " drift lines " go on to sandbanks or even dry land : the ship isn't actually going to drift! At 5 knots she can go 15 miles through the water in 3 hours. Therefore, with the dividers open to 15 miles (to whatever scale is used) and one point on C_3, mark D, where the other point cuts the track A–B to be made good. CO (parallel to C_3–D) is the direction in which the ship must be headed to reach D at the end of three hours and her average speed will be one-third of the length A–D.

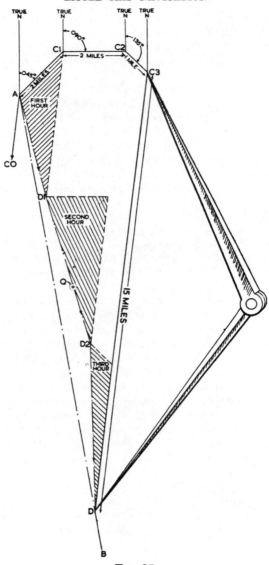

FIG. 35.

Caution. The method of applying several periods of a *varying* stream together, as described in the last paragraph, needs a little caution in use, because although it correctly gives the initial and final positions (A and D) of the ship, the track followed over the land is not actually along the straight line (A–D). Because the stream varies, the ship will actually move along the track A D_1 D_2 D as given by three current triangles, one for each hour. These three triangles are shown shaded in Fig. 35. In nine cases out of ten the fact that the ship actually reaches D via D_1 and D_2 does not matter, but in the tenth case it might. For example, if there were rocks at Q, it would be just too bad! If, therefore, you are forced to navigate really close to dangers, draw a triangle for each separate, different tidal stream, even if it means a triangle for each hour. The need, however, will very seldom arise.

CHAPTER XI

BEATING TO WINDWARD: A TACKING GADGET: GYBE-TACKING

Under sail with a foul wind it is naturally not possible to proceed along the chosen track, and the problem which then confronts the navigator involves two questions: which tack to start on and when to change tacks. The answers to these questions can be stated, in general terms, as follows:

Always start on that tack which, taking leeway and tidal stream into account, results in a course made good which lies nearer to the chosen track, and (sea room permitting) remain on it until the other tack will reach your intended destination or until the wind or stream change so as to make the course made good on the other tack lie nearer the chosen track.

Assuming constant conditions of wind, stream, and state of sea, nothing is to be gained by making a series of short tacks: two long tacks are no longer in distance than a couple of dozen short ones, and because the ship loses something every time she goes about, will take rather less time. Of course, in practice, especially when coasting, a number of short tacks may offer special advantages; for example, in keeping out of a strong foul stream, or in taking advantage of local on-shore or off-shore winds, or in keeping in smoother water, and so on. Again, an anticipated change of wind may make it inadvisable to stay as long on one tack as the above general rule would indicate. These, however, are special considerations about which it is impossible to generalise; the general rule is as above stated, and it will be obvious that to apply the rule involves, simply, the construction of current triangles for each tack.

Courses for Beating. The courses to be steered when beating are determined for you by the direction of the wind. The average modern little ship, under plain sail, is full and by about 50° off the wind, and in these circumstances will make about 5° leeway. To simplify the present explanation assume these are the performance figures of a ship wishing to beat from A to the light vessel B (Fig. 36). Draw through A on the chart a line W representing the wind direction, and then set off on each side of it two other lines, P and S, each at 50° to it, to represent the courses which can be steered, full and by, on the port and starboard tacks respectively. Then draw

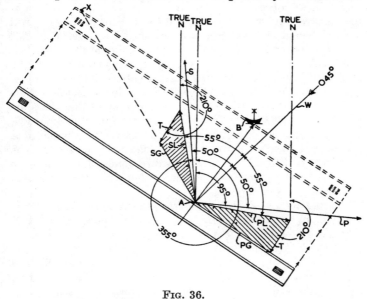

FIG. 36.

two further lines, PL and SL, at 55° to the wind line W, to represent the courses through the water (owing to leeway) on the two tacks. On each of these lines mark off, to any convenient scale, a distance to represent the ship's speed. From these points draw lines T which represent, to the same scale, the direction and speed of the tidal stream. Then the third sides, PG, SG, of these current triangles (shown shaded) will be the courses made good on the two tacks, and the one which is nearer the chosen track A–B should be the first tack adopted. Sea room permitting and special considerations apart, stay on this tack until the other tack will reach the intended destination B, or until the conditions change to make the other tack the more favourable.

In Fig. 36 the line W at 045° represents a NE wind. Sailing full and by at 50° off the wind, the ship can be headed 045+50 =095° on the port tack or 045−50=355° on the starboard tack. These ship " headings " are drawn at P and S and, corrected of course for variation and deviation, are the compass courses on the two tacks. With 5° leeway the ship will move through the water along the lines PL and SL at 55° on each side of the wind W. With a ship speed of 5 knots and a tidal stream 210°/2 knots, the courses made good on the two tacks will be PG and SG respectively, the lines T representing the tidal stream. Clearly SG makes a smaller angle with AB than does PG, so the first tack should be the starboard tack. With the parallel rule, transfer the line PG, representing course made good on the port tack, to B and note the point X, where the rule cuts the continuation of SG. The starboard tack should be maintained (if conditions remain the same) until the point X is reached, when the other tack will enable the ship to reach B.

Tacking by Log. It will be seen from Fig. 36 that it is possible, by reading the log, to ascertain when the point X is reached, for in one hour, sailing along the line SG made good, the log reading will change by 5 miles. By using the line SG as a scale of 5 miles to measure the length AX, it is easy to find out what the log reading will be at X and to alter course accordingly. *Note particularly that, although in the figure the line SG is only about $3\frac{3}{4}$ miles long, it corresponds to a change of log reading of 5 miles.*

A Useful Tacking Gadget. When you know the performance of your ship close-hauled to windward, it is possible to save a certain amount of chart work by means of a home-made " tacking protractor," as shown in Fig. 37. This consists simply of a sector-shaped piece of wood, metal, or perspex, with three radial lines scratched on it as shown. The angle at the apex is made equal to twice the angle the ship will sail full and by off the wind, plus twice the leeway angle when so sailing. Thus, for a ship that is full and by 50° off the wind and makes 5° leeway when so sailing, the apex angle would be $(2 \times 50) + (2 \times 5) = 110°$. The lines marked " Port Tack " and " Starboard Tack " are at 5° to the radial side edges and represent ship's head on these tacks. The centre line represents wind direction. A scale of miles is marked on each radial edge ; if the scale is 1 cm. to 1 mile (a quite

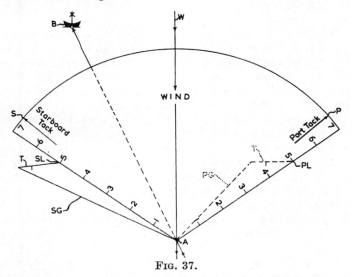

FIG. 37.

convenient scale) the whole protractor will usually be about 3 inches long, depending on the maximum estimated speed of the ship when full and by.

When it is required to start beating from A to B, draw on the chart a line W representing wind direction and passing through the ship's position A. Place the protractor on the chart with the point on position A and the central wind line over the line W. Make pencil marks at P and S. If the ship's speed is (say) 5 knots, also make marks at 5 knots on the scales, *i.e.* at PL and SL. Remove the protractor and, with the parallel rule, set off, from PL and SL, the lines T representing tidal stream, using the edge scale of the protractor to determine the lengths of these lines. In Fig. 37 a tidal stream of about 260°/1½ knots is represented by the lines T. Then the lines SG and PG represent the courses and speeds which will be made good, with a tidal stream T, when the ship is headed AS or AP on the starboard or port tack respectively. The edge scales may be used for measuring these speeds, which in the case illustrated are about 6¼ knots and 3¾ knots respectively.

This protractor will be found quite a practical gadget, because in the great majority of cases, although the ship's speed, full and by, varies with the wind strength, the angle she will sail off the wind and her leeway angle are fairly constant over wide ranges of wind strength, *provided, of course, she is always under the same amount of sail.* Obviously a " tacking protractor " prepared for a ship under plain sail will usually not be right for the same ship reefed. If desired a separate protractor may be made for the reefed condition, or by making the protractor of transparent material, it may be given extra lines for the reefed condition. Most people, however, will find the simple " plain sail " form illustrated sufficient in practice.

Gybe-Tacking. On a long passage, especially when short handed, running dead before the wind at night may give considerable anxiety unless much time is lost by shortening sail unnecessarily. In such a case, where sea room permits, considerably increased mental comfort and, indeed, speed can often be achieved by what may be called " gybe-tacking " : that is to say, by deliberately leaving the chosen track so as to bring the wind safely twenty degrees or so on one quarter, and then, after a suitable run on one tack, gybing to bring the wind on the other quarter to return to the track. In such a case it usually matters little which tack is sailed on first; in the absence of any special considerations, start on whichever tack you happen to be. It is usually convenient to remain on that tack until you change watches, when you will have the extra hands on deck for the gybe on to the next tack without disturbing the watch below. (There are bad little ship masters ; damn bad little ship masters ; and those who unnecessarily disturb the watch below !) During " gybe-tacking " the courses and distances made good are drawn out by straightforward current triangles as described in the last chapter: there will, of course, be no leeway, since the wind will be nearly aft all the time. Gybe-tacking has the advantage of reducing the risk of an involuntary gybe at night, and, although it involves an increase in the distance run, the increase is quite small and more than counter-balanced by the fact that more sail can be safely carried with resultant improved speed.

Caution. When tacking, gybe-tacking, and running, the cautious navigator will expect considerable differences between the courses he has ordered and the courses actually steered, especially if there is any sea about. When close-hauled, most helmsmen tend to produce an actual course a little downwind of the one they think they are steering, especially those helmsmen who fancy themselves at " pinching a bit in the puffs." What actually happens is that, by coming too close to the wind, the ship greatly increases her leeway temporarily, loses speed gradually, and then is knocked off by the sea or has to be paid off. All these effects are down-wind effects, though the helmsman thinks he has got a bit extra to windward. In running, most helmsmen tend to average a course a little " away from the boom," i.e. with the wind and sea on the port quarter the course is apt to be a little too much to port. If you don't " know " your helmsman (and it is almost certain he will not " know " himself), have a pipe or two with him during his watch and keep an observant but unobtrusive eye on the compass, the wake, and the speed of the water past the counter. All navigational errors, are, of course, entirely due to the navigator—never to the helms-man. All the same, it is sometimes instructive for a navigator to watch his helmsman at work.

CHAPTER XII

POSITION LINES AND FIXES: COMPASS AND TRANSITS

The cautious navigator loses no opportunity of fixing his position as often and as accurately as possible, even if he is merely coasting a few miles off shore or is within a few miles of a harbour which he is making for and can, perhaps, already discern. Changes in weather conditions can, and often do, make a few miles last many hours, so that precise knowledge of the ship's position at all times is important to her safety—to say nothing of the navigator's peace of mind. Indeed it is no exaggeration to say that frequent, accurate position-finding is more important to the little ship—especially the little ship under sail—than to the big one, for the little ship cannot anchor in many places where her larger sister can " wait for it." The sudden onset of fog or really heavy rain often imposes on the little ship navigator urgent problems whose satisfactory solution depends on a precise knowledge of position. To take an example at random, a little ship unlucky enough to be caught by sudden evening fog when nearing Dover towards the end of a cross-Channel passage would give her navigator plenty to worry about if all he knew was that he had " seen the S. Goodwin LV ahead and to starboard about a quarter of an hour ago." The navigator who, as a matter of ordinary routine, had fixed his position as soon as he could, would be much better placed both to keep off the Goodwins and out of the way of steamer traffic into and out of the Downs.

Straight and Circular Position Lines. In general, a single observation of a known fixed mark gives a POSITION LINE: that is to say, defines a line on which the ship must be at the time of the observation. A position line may be straight or circular, depending upon how it is taken. The compass is the usual means of obtaining a straight position line; the sextant the usual means of obtaining a circular one. In this chapter, methods of obtaining and using straight position lines by compass and transits will be described, the obtaining and utilisation of circular position lines by sextant forming the main subject of the next chapter.

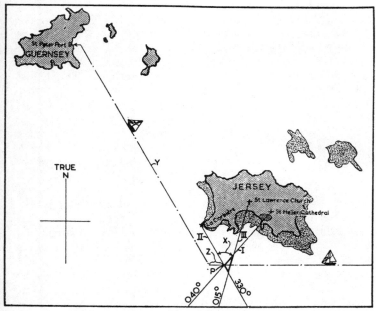

FIG. 38.

Single Compass Bearing. The simplest and commonest form of straight position line is that given by a single compass bearing. A bearing of some visible known object, shown on the chart, is taken and, after correction for variation and (if necessary) deviation, is drawn as a line on the chart. Then the ship must be somewhere on that line at the time the bearing is taken. Fig. 38 gives a typical illustration of a position line by compass bearing. Here a ship, bound past

Jersey to St. Peter Port, Guernsey, takes a compass bearing of the Cathedral, St. Helier, Jersey. This bearing, corrected for variation and deviation, is 040° true. Accordingly a pencil line I, extending in the direction 040°–220°, is drawn on the chart through the cross representing the Cathedral. The ship's position is somewhere on this line at the time the bearing is taken.

Fix by Crossed Bearings. Obviously, if two intersecting position lines can be obtained at the same time, the ship must be on both of them and the point of intersection must be the ship's position: in other words a FIX is obtained. The simplest form of fix is by simultaneous crossed bearings. This is also illustrated in Fig. 38. Suppose that simultaneously with the bearing of St. Helier Cathedral, La Corbière lighthouse was found to bear (after correction for variation and deviation) 330° true. A second pencil line II, extending 330°–150° through La Corbière, is drawn on the chart. The point P where these lines intersect is the position of the ship.

In practice, in a little ship, it is usually impossible, for obvious reasons, to take two bearings simultaneously. If, however, they are taken with reasonable expedition one after the other, any error due to ship's movement between the bearings will be negligible. The object whose bearing is changing the more rapidly should be observed first, i.e. the one which is more nearly abeam, or, if they are widely different distances away, the nearer one. The best condition for obtaining a fix by cross bearings is when the bearings are at right angles to one another, for then any error in taking either bearing has least effect on the accuracy of the fix. Quite a reliable fix in normal conditions of sea can be obtained, however, if the angle X between the bearings is 45° or more. If the angle X is less than 30°, the fix obtained should be regarded with considerable suspicion : indeed it is doubtful whether a fix by cross bearings with so small an " angle of cut " is worth taking at all in a little ship (except perhaps in a really smooth sea), because any errors in the bearings will produce large errors in the fix.

Cocked Hat. It often happens that a third cross bearing can be taken and when this is available it should always be observed and plotted. Referring again to Fig. 38 a third bearing III (corrected) of 015° true, has been taken of St. Lawrence Church and plotted on the chart. If all three bearings are taken simultaneously, and with theoretically perfect accuracy, they will all intersect at the same point. In practice, of course, this never happens and the crossing lines define a triangle, known as a COCKED HAT, such as that shown in heavy lines in Fig. 38. The position of the ship is somewhere in this triangle, the most probable position being nearer that corner at which the bearings most nearly at right angles cross one another (in Fig. 38 bearings I and II). The principal value of the third bearing is to serve as a check to the other two, the size of the cocked hat giving an indication of the accuracy of the bearing observations. If the cocked hat is a large one the errors are large and fresh bearings should be taken.

Transferred Position Lines. If the course and distance *made good over the ground* after obtaining a position line are known, that line may be moved correspondingly on the chart and made use of in its new position. Referring again to Fig. 38, suppose the ship had been steering W at the time the three crossed bearings were taken and the navigator had decided that the track Y at 330° was a safe line to St. Peter Port, clearing all dangers after passing Jersey. Then, by reading the log when the bearing of La Corbière (330°) was taken, and continuing to sail W until the log gave a new reading such that the difference of the two readings was equal to the length of the line Z on the chart, the ship's course could then be altered to 330° in the secure knowledge that she was now correctly headed up the track Y. In this example, for the sake of simplicity, it has been assumed that there is no tidal stream or leeway. The line Z is obviously the course and distance made good *over the ground* and these will be the same respectively as the course steered and the difference of the log readings if, and only if, there is no leeway or tidal stream. These factors, if they exist, must be taken into account, as already described in an earlier chapter, in estimating the course and distance made good over the ground between the taking of the actual bearing of La Corbière and the transference of the position line thus obtained to coincide with the desired new track Y.

Running Fix. The transferred position line also forms the basis of the RUNNING FIX, which is a fix obtained by crossing a

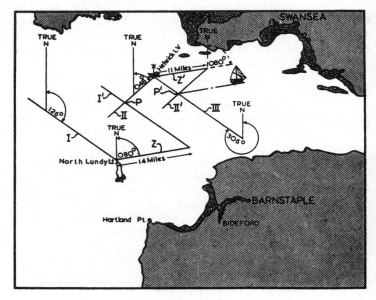

FIG. 39.

position line with another one obtained earlier and transferred. In the running fix, a bearing is taken of an object to give a position line, the ship is steered to make good a known course and distance until a second object is seen, a bearing is taken of the second object, and the second position line thus obtained is crossed with the first position line transferred by the course and distance made good. Fig. 39 gives a practical example of a running fix of this nature.

Here a ship steering 080° true up the Bristol Channel takes a bearing of N. Lundy Light, the log then reading 53·6. This bearing (corrected for variation and deviation) is 126° true. The ship is therefore somewhere on position line I. Two hours later Helwick LV is observed bearing 048° true. The ship is, therefore, then somewhere on position line II. Suppose the ship has a fair stream of 2 knots under her and that the log reads 63·6 at the time of the second bearing. Then, between the two bearings, she will have made good a distance of 14 miles in a direction 080° true, 10 miles (63·6—53·6), being due to her own movement, and 4 miles being due to two hours of a 2-knot tidal stream. If, therefore, a line Z be drawn through N. Lundy Light in a direction 080°, and 14 miles long, the position line I can be drawn transferred (i.e. parallel to itself) at I' through the end of the line Z, and the point P, where this transferred line I' cuts the line II, will be the ship's position at the time of the second bearing.

Running Fix by Two Bearings of the Same Object. There is also a form of running fix in which two observations are taken of the same object. Again the course and distance made good between the two observations must be known. Suppose in Fig. 39 that the Lundy Island bearing I had been missed, but the Helwick LV bearing giving position line II had been taken, the log reading then being, as already stated, 63·6. Suppose also that, as before, the ship is steering 080° with a fair tidal stream of 2 knots under her, and that 1½ hours later, when the log reads 71·6, Helwick LV bears 306° true. Then, at the time of the last bearing, the ship will be on position line III, and during the interval between the two bearings, will have made good over the ground 11 miles (71·6—63·6=8, plus 3 miles due to tidal stream) in a direction 080° true. If, therefore, a line Z', 11 miles long, is drawn in a direction 080° through Helwick LV, and the position line II is transferred to II' through the end of line Z', the point P' where it cuts position line III, will be the ship's position at the time of the last bearing.

Change of Angle on Bow. As a ship on a fixed course approaches an object so as to pass it at a distance, the angle at which that object appears on the bow gradually increases until it is abeam. This fact forms the basis of another useful running fix known as DISTANCE BY CHANGE OF BEARING. By taking two successive bearings of an object before it is abeam, and noting the distance made good between the bearings, the distance away at the second bearing may be looked up directly in the table entitled " Distance by Change of Bearing " to be found e.g. in *Inman's Tables*. Part of this table is reproduced in

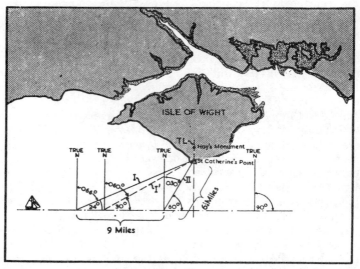

FIG. 40.

Appendix 4 and should be referred to in following the example illustrated in Fig. 40.

In this figure a ship proceeding up Channel on a course 090° true, first sights St. Catherine's Point light bearing 066° true (position line I, Fig. 40). The light is therefore 090−066=24° on the port bow. The log reading is 81. An hour and a half later, the log then reading 91·5, a second bearing of the light is taken and found to be 030° (position line II). The light is therefore now 090−030=60° on the port bow. Suppose the ship has a foul 1 knot tidal stream against her. Then the miles run between the two bearings is 9, being 91·5—81=10·5 due to the ship's own movement through the water, less 1½ miles due to the foul tidal stream. Entering the table (Appendix 4) with " Angle from Bow at First Bearing " 24 at the top of the table and " Change of Bearing " 36 (60—24) at the side, we get the miles distant at the second bearing for each mile of run to be 0·69. As the miles run are 9, the distance off, along the second bearing line II, is 9 ×0·69=6¼ miles (near enough).

Caution. The method of distance by change of bearing obviously depends for its accuracy on a correct knowledge of the distance run between bearings. The method may therefore be safely used if there is no tidal stream or if the stream is dead fair, or dead foul or nearly so. *It should not be used if there is any material cross stream or much leeway.*

Doubling the Angle on the Bow. A special case of the method of distance by change of bearing which does not involve the use of tables is that known as DOUBLING THE ANGLE ON THE BOW. From elementary geometry it will be seen that if the bearings are so chosen that the angle on the bow at the second bearing is exactly twice that at the first, the distance away at the second bearing is the same as the distance run between bearings. Refer again to Fig. 40. If the first bearing taken of St. Catherine's light had been that shown dotted at I' with the light 060° true (30° on the port bow), and the course 090° had been maintained until the light bore 030° true (60° on the port bow), the distance away at the second bearing would clearly be equal to the distance made good between the two bearings, because the triangle made by the two bearing lines I' and II and the ship's track is isosceles. As in the case of the method of distance by change of bearing, the method of distance by doubling the angle on the bow may be used with a stream which is dead fair or foul (or nearly so)—*never with any material cross stream or leeway.*

Four-Point Bearing. This is a special and very convenient case of the method of doubling the angle on the bow. If an object is observed bearing 4 points (45°) on the bow and the ship's course is maintained until it is abeam (90° on the bow), then, obviously; the angle on the bow has been doubled, and, as before, the distance away at the second bearing—when the object is abeam—is equal to the distance run between bearings. Once again the method is satisfactory with a dead fair or foul stream—*not with a cross stream or leeway*. The advantage of the four-point bearing is that it gives the distance off abeam— often convenient. Its defect is that it does not give a fix until the ship is at her nearest to the object, which may be a headland with outlying dangers such as rocks.

General Caution. Transits. Any position line or fix obtained with the aid of the compass will be subject to the errors of observation inherent in the taking of a compass bearing. In a little ship in a seaway such errors may not only be substantial in themselves, but in different directions for two successive bearings, thus introducing into a fix an error larger than that in either bearing. Therefore, if the ship is bobbing about badly *do not trust compass bearings too far*, and check or replace position lines found by the compass by position lines found in some other, more accurate way. One such other way, requiring more practice than that necessary to use the compass, but usually giving more reliable results if it can be used at all, is by the aid of the sextant. This will be described in the next chapter. Another way, which is both easier to practise and almost entirely free from error, is by taking advantage of transits of objects marked on the chart. When two objects come into line they are said to be IN TRANSIT. Most reliable position lines can be derived from transits. Thus, referring again to Fig. 40, there is, inland of St. Catherine's light, an easily identifiable conspicuous object, namely, Hoy's Monument. If a line joining this Monument and St. Catherine's light be drawn on the chart it will be seen to extend in a direction 356—176° true. The navigator of the ship in Fig. 40 could therefore replace the compass position line II of that figure by the transit position line TL with considerable improvement in accuracy. All he would have to do, after taking the first bearing I of St. Catherine's light and reading the log, would be to continue on his course of 090° until the Monument and the light appeared in line, when he would read the log again and take the bearing TL directly off the chart. A position line taken by a transit in this way may be used for any purpose for which a compass position line can be used.

Identification of Objects in Transit. Transit position lines are probably the most easily obtained and reliable of all, and should be used wherever available. An intelligent examination of the chart prior to a coastal passage will usually reveal quite a number of valuable transit lines. The only difficulty sometimes presented is that of identifying the objects in transit, but this difficulty can almost always be solved with the aid of the compass. Reverting once more to Fig. 40, suppose that Hoy's Monument was not—as in fact it is— an isolated monument, but merely one of three pillar-like erections standing up in different places from the general body of buildings in a town, so that a navigator who had never seen it before might have difficulty in identifying which of the three it was. By taking a bearing of each erection in turn just before it came into line with St. Catherine's light, he would be able to determine which of them was Hoy's Monument, because only that one would give the correct bearing as indicated by the chart (356° in the present example) when in transit with the light. This trick of identifying objects by compass is particularly useful in those numerous cases in which one of the objects on a transit line is only one of several generally similar churches in different parts of a town.

Running Fixes and Tidal Streams. In any running fix—*i.e.* any form of fix which depends upon two position lines with a run between—any error in the estimation of the run between will be reflected in the fix obtained. It is therefore important not to neglect a tidal stream, since this is one component of the " run between." In transferring a position line a tidal stream, whether fair, foul or cross, can be directly allowed for in the ordinary way by drawing the " run between " as two lines in succession, namely, a line representing ship's movement, with a line representing stream drawn from its end. In the majority of practical instances, however, running fixes will be used when coasting, when nine times out of ten the stream will be either dead fair or dead foul. In such cases the stream movement need not be drawn out but simply added to or subtracted from the ship's movement, as in the examples in this chapter. Where, however, there is a cross stream—as in a cross-Channel passage—it should be carefully estimated from the information given on the chart, or in a tidal atlas, and properly allowed for in transferring a position line, by drawing out as in an ordinary current triangle.

CHAPTER XIII

POSITION LINES AND FIXES: SEXTANT METHODS: STATION POINTER

General Principle. The angle subtended at the eye by an object depends upon how far away it is from the observer, the greater the distance the smaller being the angle. If, therefore, the height of an object, such as a lighthouse, is known and the angle subtended by it is measured with the sextant, it is a matter of elementary calculation to find out how far away it is. Since all points at the same distance from an object are on a circle having that object as centre and that distance as radius, measurement of the subtended angle gives a circular position line on which the observer must be. Fig. 41a is a sketch-chart of Dungeness and Fig. 41b is a view of this headland with a ship rounding the point. If the height H of the lighthouse lantern above sea-level be known, the distance D of the ship can be obtained by measuring the angle A with the sextant. As will be obvious, H and D are the two perpendicular sides of a right-angled triangle and, by ordinary trigonometry, the distance D is equal to the height H multiplied by the cotangent of the angle A. The position line on which the ship must be, is therefore a circle (Fig. 41a) with the lighthouse as centre and D as radius.

> *Example.* A ship off Dungeness takes a vertical sextant angle on the lighthouse lantern. If the height of the lantern above sea-level is 130 ft. and the angle is $0° 21' 00''$, how far off is the ship? Cotangent $21'$ (from *Inman's Tables* or any other mathematical tables)$=163\cdot7$.

$$\therefore \text{ Distance}=163\cdot7\times130 \text{ ft.}=\frac{163\cdot7\times130}{3} \text{ yds.}$$

$$=7,093 \text{ yds.}$$
$$=3 \text{ miles } 5\tfrac{1}{2} \text{ cables (very nearly).}$$

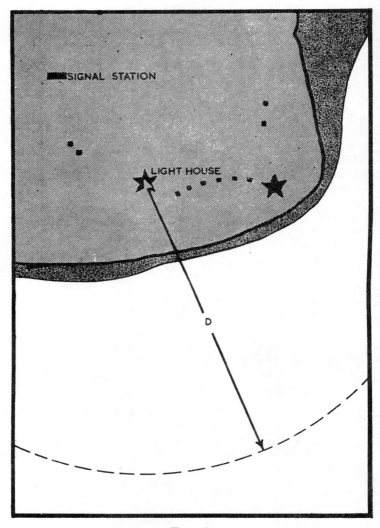

SIGNAL STATION

LIGHT HOUSE

D

FIG. 41a.

Mast Head Angles. If Tables are carried, all calculation can in most cases be avoided by using a " mast head angles " table. An excerpt from such tables is given in Appendix 5, from which it will be seen that the distance (in yards) at the side of the table can be taken out directly (interpolating,

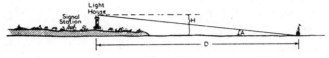

FIG. 41b.

if necessary, by eye), by entering the appropriate nearest height column and reading down the column to the nearest tabulated angle. Thus, using these tables (see Appendix 5) for the above example, and entering the height column headed 129 ft. (the nearest to the height of 130 ft.), we obtain opposite 0° 21·1' (the nearest to the measured angle of 21') the distance of 7,000 yds.—which is near enough for most practical navigational purposes without interpolating.

565 Rule. The same calculation can be done without tables, to a degree of accuracy which is near enough for most little ship purposes, by the so-called 565 rule of the seaman. By this rule, the distance off in miles is equal to 0·565 times the height of the object in feet, divided by the sextant angle in minutes. Taking the same example again by the 565 rule we get :

$$\text{Distance in miles} = \frac{0·565 \times 130}{21} = 3·5 \text{ miles (very nearly).}$$

Half-and-Half Rule. An adaptation of the 565 rule, which has the advantage of giving easier arithmetic and is nearly as accurate (it gives the distance about 3 per cent. less than the 565 rule) is the HALF-AND-HALF rule. By this rule add 1/20th of the height of the object to ½ the height and divide the sum by the angle in minutes. The answer is (near enough for most purposes) the distance in miles. 1/20th is, of course, the same as ½ with the decimal point moved along one figure—hence the name *half-and-half*. Once more taking the same example, this time by the half-and-half rule, we get :

One-half the height (130 ft)   65

One-twentieth the height   6·5

Sum $\overline{71·5}$

Distance in miles $= \dfrac{71·5}{21} =$ (a little more than) 3·4 miles.

1.2.3 Rule. For heights in metres the distance off can be easily calculated with an accuracy of about 1% by this simple and original rule. Add together the height in metres, half that height, and one third that height (1,2,3) and divide the sum by the sextant angle in minutes. The result is the distance off in sea miles.

Example. Height in metres 26 metres: Sextant angle 14 minutes. Required the distance off.

Height	=26
Half the height	=13
One third the height	= 8·6
Divide by 14	47·6
Distance off	3·4 sea miles.

Finding the Height. Tide Allowance. The heights of light-houses and numerous headlands and hills in coastal areas are obtainable from many sources, notably the charts, the light lists, and the pilot books. As already stated, all such heights as given on the chart are heights above the level of H.W. springs, and strictly speaking, therefore, unless it is H.W. springs when a vertical sextant angle is taken, the height as given on the chart should be increased (for purposes of cal-culation of distance) by the amount by which the sea-level at the time is below the level of H.W. springs. In many cases, however, the height of the object is so much larger than the fall of the tide below H.W. springs that the inaccuracy involved in neglecting tidal fall can be tolerated. In prac-tically all cases a quite rough correction for height of tide will be amply sufficient. It is worth remembering that, if tide is ignored, any error introduced thereby will make the distance away appear less than it really is, so that, for some purposes at any rate, such an error may be regarded as " on the safe side."

Heights of Lighthouses. The heights of lighthouses as given on the chart are taken to the centre of the lantern—not to the top of the lighthouse. In " bringing down " a lighthouse to sea-level with the sextant, therefore, it is the centre of the lantern which should be brought down to the sea, *not* the top of the lighthouse. In practice this hardly ever presents the slightest difficulty, it being quite easy to judge by eye, with adequate accuracy for good little ship navigation, where the lantern is. Some people prefer, however, always to bring the top of the lighthouse down to the sea. In such cases the height used for calculation purposes should be increased by the difference in level between the lantern and the top. This difference is 14 ft. for a first-power light, 8 ft. for a fourth-power light, and may be taken as 10 ft. for a second or third-power light. If this difference is ignored the error will, as in the case of ignoring tide, make the calculated distance less than the actual distance.

Vertical Danger Angle. A most useful variation of the vertical sextant angle is the so-called VERTICAL DANGER ANGLE. Suppose it is desired to round a headland at a predetermined safe distance—for example, to keep clear of unmarked off-lying rocks or a race. The sextant angle corresponding to this distance is calculated in advance and set on the sextant. Then, as the headland is rounded, the sextant is picked up from time to time and, without altering its setting, the headland is observed. So long as the angle set on the sextant is too large to bring the top of the headland up to the sea, the ship is more than the required distance off. As soon as the headland comes up to the sea, however, the ship is at the minimum pre-determined distance and course should be altered to haul off.

Example. Proceeding to the westward from Poole, a ship desires to pass Anvil Point at a minimum distance of

3 miles to clear St. Albans Race. Anvil Point Lighthouse is 150 ft. above H.W.O.S. What angle should be set on the sextant (assuming no index error) for use as a vertical danger angle?

Since a minimum distance off is required, tide can be ignored, since any error on this account will only result in the ship's distance off being a little increased.

Using the 565 rule the required angle is $\dfrac{0 \cdot 565 \times 150}{3} = 28 \cdot 3'$.

Caution. Referring again to Fig. 41b it will be seen that the assumption behind vertical sextant angle calculations is that the triangle with H as one side and D as another is right angled. In practice this is not strictly true, in part because the eye of the observer is a little above sea-level and some-times because the object observed is some distance inshore.

Normally, the triangle actually taken is so nearly right angled that error from this cause is entirely negligible, but occasionally cases do arise where it is inadvisable to use the method. These cases are where the distance away from the shore is small and the object observed is well inland. Fig. 42 illustrates a bad case in which the cautious navigator would not rely upon a vertical sextant angle. Here it will be apparent that the angle A actually measured is considerably different from the angle B upon which the calculation of D is based. It will also be apparent from Fig. 42 that *the nearer the observer is*

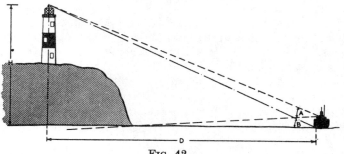

FIG. 42.

to sea-level, the less will the error be. Accordingly, with a little ship, the occasions when a vertical sextant angle will lead to appreciable error will be few and far between and ordinary common sense is sufficient to guard against those cases.

Index Error. If the sextant has any index error (see Chapter VIII) this should, of course, be applied to any single instrument reading. Many navigators, however, prefer to measure angles twice, once " on the arc " and once " off the arc." If this be done and the mean of the two readings be taken, the answer will be free of index error because it cancels out. Thus if a sextant having an index error of $+1'$ be used to measure an angle which is really $21'$, the reading " on the arc " will be $20'$ and the reading " off the arc " will be $22'$, giving a correct mean reading of $21'$. This method has the advantage of giving an automatic check on accuracy of observation, because the two readings should differ by twice the index error, which is (or should be) known.

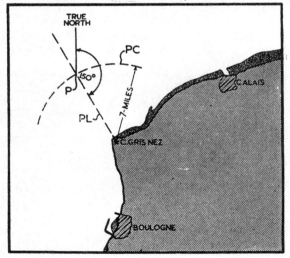

Fig. 43.

Fix by Crossed Sextant Angle and Compass Bearing or Transit. One of the best, simplest, and most useful of all fixes, and one much neglected by little ships, is that obtained by taking a compass bearing and a vertical sextant angle of the same object. The compass bearing gives a straight position line which is radial to the object, while the sextant gives a circular position line having the object as centre. These two position lines are, therefore, at right angles to one another—the ideal "cut." An example of this fix is given with reference to Fig. 43.

Example. A ship bound for Calais finds Cap Gris Nez light to bear 150° true. A sextant angle (index error −1′) gives 19·8′ on the arc and 17·8′ off the arc. The height of Cap Gris Nez light is 233 ft. Plot the ship's position.

$$\text{Sextant angle} \quad = \quad \frac{19\cdot8 + 17\cdot8}{2} \quad = \quad 18\cdot8' \text{ (checked correct since index error is } -1')$$

$$\therefore \text{ distance off} \quad = \quad \frac{0\cdot565 \times 233}{18\cdot8} \quad = \quad \text{(very nearly) } 7 \text{ miles.}$$

With radius of 7 miles and centre on Cap Gris Nez, draw the arc of the position circle PC. Also draw the position line

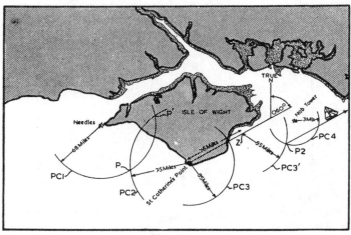

Fig. 44.

PL given by the bearing. The ship's position is at P—an excellent fix. In this example tide has been neglected, for owing to the height of Cap Gris Nez it could, in any case, only introduce a minor correction.

A very similar and even more satisfactory fix can be obtained by crossing a vertical sextant angle with a transit. Thus, referring back to Fig. 40, a vertical sextant angle taken on St. Catherine's Point light when it was in transit with Hoy's Monument (line TL of Fig. 40) would give an excellent fix, the transit giving a straight position line and the sextant angle giving a position circle cutting it at right angles.

Fix by Two Sextant Angles. A fix can be obtained by crossing position circles obtained by two vertical sextant angles, just as by crossing position lines obtained by two bearings or transits. Fig. 44 illustrates a fix of this nature. Here, simultaneous vertical sextant angles of the Needles light and St. Catherine's Point light give the former as 6·8 miles distant and the latter as 7·5 miles away. Two circles, PC1, PC2, with centres at the Needles and St. Catherine's, and radii of 6·8 miles and 7·5 miles respectively, are drawn. Their point of intersection, P, is the ship's position. This method of obtaining fixes by the sextant, though requiring considerably more practice than by crossed compass bearings, is in most cases a good deal more reliable and accurate if weather conditions are good enough to allow the method to be used at all. With a little practice a fix such as that illustrated in Fig. 44 can be readily taken in what is officially termed a " moderate" sea—which is what most little ships regard as rough—and is much to be preferred to crossed compass bearings taken under the same conditions.

It will be noted from Fig. 44 that the position circles cross at two points P, P', only one of which is correct. In practice there is never any difficulty in selecting the correct " cut "— in the illustrated example the other is some miles inland— either by eye or by taking a rough compass bearing of one of the objects.

As with the case of a fix by crossed bearings, a fix by crossed position circles is most reliable when the objects are at right angles as observed from the ship, and as the angle between them gets more and more acute or obtuse the effects of errors of observation get larger and larger.

Transferred Position Circles. A position circle can be transferred and used, for example, for a running fix, in much the same way as a position line. Fig. 44 illustrates this also. Here, a ship sailing 060° true, takes a vertical sextant angle of St. Catherine's light when on the port quarter, and finds the distance off to be 5·5 miles, giving position circle PC3. An hour and a half later, during which time the ship has made good 7·5 miles 060°, an angle on the Nab Tower makes its distance to be 3 miles, giving position circle PC4. Through St. Catherine's a line is drawn in a direction 060°, and a distance of 7·5 miles is set off along it to the point Z. The centre of circle PC3 is transferred to Z, and the transferred circle PC3', of 5·5 miles radius, drawn in its new position. The point P2, where PC3' cuts PC4, is the ship's position at the time the Nab Tower observation is taken.

Horizontal Sextant Angles. When two identifiable objects marked on the chart are in sight, a very reliable position circle can be obtained, even though the heights of the objects are not known, by using the sextant to measure the horizontal angle between them; that is to say by holding the sextant horizontally and adjusting it until the reflected image of one object coincides with the direct image of the other. This HORIZONTAL SEXTANT ANGLE method, as it is called, is based on the facts that any three points must lie on the circumference of a circle, and all the angles in a segment of a circle are equal. If, therefore, the horizontal angle subtended at a ship by two points ashore is measured, it is possible, by simple geometry, to draw the circle which passes through both shore points and the ship, whose position must therefore be somewhere on that circle. Fig. 45 illustrates a typical case of a position circle by horizontal sextant angle. In this figure, a ship proceeding northwards along the French coast takes a horizontal sextant angle of the end of the southern arm of Boulogne breakwater and the Fort at Ambleteuse, finding it 60°. The geometrical construction for finding the position

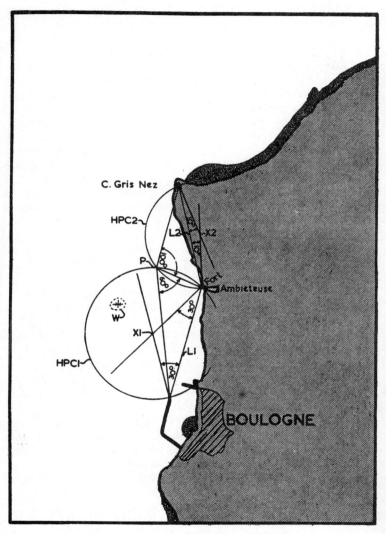

Fig. 45.

circle HPC1, passing through the ship and the two shore objects and to include the measured angle of 60°, is as follows: draw a straight line L1 between the two shore objects, and from each end of it lay off the complement of the measured angle. The complement of an angle being 90° minus the angle, in this case angles of 30° (90 − 60) are laid off at each end. If the measured angle is less than 90° (the illustrated case) the complementary angles are laid off towards the ship, as shown. If the measured angle is more than 90°, 90° is subtracted from it and the remainder laid off away from the ship, *i.e.* on the other side of the line L1. Where the radii of the complementary angles cross, at X1, is the centre of the position circle HPC1, on which the ship must be.

Horizontal Danger Angle. A predetermined horizontal sextant angle may be used to maintain a desired minimum distance off shore in much the same way as a vertical danger angle. Thus, in Fig. 45, suppose it was desired to clear the wreck W by a certain distance. A circle would be drawn through Fort Ambleteuse and Boulogne breakwater so as to enclose the wreck by the required distance. Any point in this circle (which might be the circle HPC1), is then joined to the Fort and to the breakwater, and the angle at this point measured and set on the sextant. From time to time the Fort and breakwater are observed through the sextant, held horizontally. So long as the angle set on the instrument is too small to bring the reflected and direct images, respectively, of these two objects together, the ship is at more than the required distance. If, however, the images come together, course should be altered to haul off.

Fix by Two Horizontal Sextant Angles. Two such horizontal sextant angles, requiring a minimum of three recognisable objects ashore, will give two intersecting position circles, and therefore a fix. This also is illustrated in Fig. 45. Simultaneously with the angle of 60° between Boulogne breakwater and Ambleteuse Fort, the angle between the Fort and Cap Gris Nez is measured and found to be 100°. The line L2 between these points is drawn as before, and angles of 10° (100 − 90) are laid off shorewards from its ends (shorewards because the measured angle exceeds 90°) to give X2, the centre of the second position circle HPC2. The point P where the circles intersect is the ship's position.

Station Pointer. A fix by two horizontal sextant angles taken on three objects, as in Fig. 45, may be plotted on the chart without geometrical construction by means of an instrument known as the STATION POINTER, an example of which is shown in Plate VII. It consists of a circular protractor I, marked out in degrees along its edge and having a small central hole or pricker H, a fixed radial arm FR, and two movable radial arms, MR1 and MR2, pivoted at the centre of the protractor, one each side of the fixed arm. When two horizontal sextant angles have been taken on three objects, as in Fig. 45, the movable arms are adjusted until one angle is between the fixed arm and one movable arm, and the other is between the fixed arm and the other movable arm. The instrument is then placed on the chart and moved about until the reading edges of the three arms pass through the representations of the three objects, taking care, of course, that the correct angles are between the correct pairs of objects. The centre of the protractor is then in the ship's position, which may be marked off on the chart with a pencil or pricker.

Tracing-Paper or Celluloid as Station Pointer. If a station pointer is not carried, a similar result can be obtained by using tracing-paper, drawing three lines at the two correct angles on it, and then moving the paper over the chart until the lines pass through the representations of the three objects, the meeting point of the three lines being then pricked through on the chart. A large celluloid protractor with one surface slightly matted or roughened so that it will take pencil markings which can subsequently be rubbed out, is still more convenient than tracing paper. If that excellent and well-known substitute for a parallel rule in a little ship, the Douglas protractor, is carried, it is ideal for this (among other) uses, the central hole, the edge degree markings and the matted surface for taking temporary pencil markings, rendering it most convenient for employment as a station pointer.

Horizontal Sextant Angle Fixes. Caution. A careful consideration of Fig. 45 will show that there is one condition in which a fix by two horizontal sextant angles on three shore objects is unsatisfactory—namely, when the three shore objects and the ship all lie on, or nearly on, the circumference of a common circle. It is not a common condition, but it does sometimes arise, and when it does the method should not be used. It is, perhaps, more convenient to remember the conditions when the method can be safely used. They are :

1. When the three shore objects are more or less in a straight line.

2. When the middle of the three objects is on the ship's side of a line joining the outer objects.

3. When the ship is inside a triangle formed by the three objects.

4. When the ship is on or near a line joining the two outer objects.

5. When the three objects are on a curve which is concave as viewed from the ship, but the ship is well outside the circle passing through the three objects.

Sextant v. Compass. Although sextant methods of fixing the position involve more skill and (usually) more chart work than compass methods, and are therefore less commonly favoured by many little ships, the generally superior accuracy and reliability of sextant observations over compass observations render it well worth while to persevere until automatic proficiency is obtained. The sextant carefully and proficiently used is to a large extent immune from errors due to the ship jumping about in a seaway ; the compass is not. The difficulty with the sextant is not that of obtaining an accurate reading so much as that of being able to hold the instrument " on " and obtaining a reading at all. With a little experience it becomes possible, when a sextant reading has been taken, to " know " whether it is a good one or not—an invaluable advantage. With the compass it is much easier to obtain some sort of reading and distressingly easy, under bad conditions, to obtain readings which are in serious and often quite unsuspected error. The commonly encountered prejudice against the use of the sextant in little ships is largely nonsense; the " old hand " who says that the sextant " is all right for a liner but no good for 10 tons " would generally be more truthful if he said, " I did try it once or twice, got silly results, and was too proud to try again."

CHAPTER XIV

OTHER AIDS TO POSITION FINDING: FOG NAVIGATION

Distance of Sea Horizon. Knowledge of the distance of the sea horizon is often of considerable assistance in obtaining a fix. If a navigation light—for example, of a light vessel—is brought just to " dip " under the horizon, the distance of the ship from the light is obviously the sum of the distances of the ship to the horizon and the light to the horizon. This is shown in Fig. 46, in which a ship and a light vessel are so

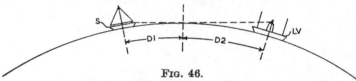

FIG. 46.

situated that the light can just be seen on the horizon when viewed from the ship. Clearly the distance from ship S to light vessel LV is equal to the sum of the respective distances to the horizon, *i.e.* to D1+D2.

The distance of any object to the visible horizon depends, of course, upon its height above sea-level. The easiest way to find the distance is from a " DISTANCE OF THE SEA HORIZON " table. A portion of such a table is reproduced in Appendix 6.

> *Example.* The light of the Kentish Knock LV (height 40 ft.) is observed just to dip on the horizon when viewed from deck with the eye 10 ft. above the sea. How far off is the LV?

From Appendix 6:

Distance of sea horizon for height of 40 ft.= 7·26 miles.

    ,,   ,,   ,,   ,,   ,,   10 ft.= 3·63   ,,

    Required distance=10·89   ,,

Calculation of Distance of Sea Horizon. If tables are not available the distance of the sea horizon, in miles, may be calculated with sufficient accuracy for normal navigation, by extracting the square root of the height in feet and multiplying by $\frac{8}{7}$. The closeness of accuracy obtained will be seen by working the last example by this method and comparing with the results given by Appendix 6:

Distance of sea horizon for height of 40 ft.

$$=\tfrac{8}{7}\sqrt{40}=\tfrac{8}{7}\times 6\cdot32=7\cdot22 \text{ miles}$$

Distance of sea horizon for height of 10 ft.

$$=\tfrac{8}{7}\sqrt{10}=\tfrac{8}{7}\times 3\cdot16=3\cdot61 \quad ,,$$

$$\text{Required distance}=\overline{10\cdot83} \quad ,,$$

The simplest way of calculating horizon distance from heights given in metres is to convert metres to feet by means of any metre/feet conversion table (there is one in Admiralty Tide Tables) and then use the above formula.

Fix by Bearing and Horizon Distance. If a bearing of a light which is observed to dip on the horizon is taken simultaneously with the observation of its distance by the above methods, a good reliable fix is obtained. The " loom " of a light at night can usually be observed at deck level long before the light itself, and it is therefore an easy matter, on approach, to climb into the rigging to a height sufficient to bring the light itself on to the horizon and then to calculate the distance and combine it with a bearing to obtain a fix.

Visibility of Lights: Range. The *Range* of a light may be given in one or more of three ways in official publications, including Admiralty charts and Light Lists—namely as *Luminous* range, *Nominal* range, or *Geographical* range. Luminous range is computed on the basis of the candle power of the light: Nominal range is the luminous range when the visibility at sea, in daylight, is 10 miles: Geographical range is calculated, not upon the power of the light, but solely upon the basis of the distance at which it can be seen on the horizon when viewed from an arbitrarily chosen height of 15 feet above the sea. In the case of any powerful, major, light, geographical range is the smallest of the three. When a light is seen exactly on the horizon, it is said to be " *dipping*," for if the height from which it is viewed is reduced, it " dips " below the horizon.

If a light is observed to dip on the horizon, it is a simple matter to calculate its distance away to a navigationally useful degree of approximation—normally to an accuracy of plus or minus half a mile—from a knowledge of its geographical range and your own height of eye. Because the geographical range is the sum of the horizon distance of the light plus the horizon distance for 15 feet, all that it is necessary to do is to apply to the geographical range a correction for your own height of eye if it is other than 15 feet. The horizon distance for 15 feet (see Appendix 6) is 4·45 miles and that for 9 feet is 3·44 miles. If therefore a light with a geographical range of 20 miles is seen to dip on the horizon from a height of 9 feet, its distance from the observer is $20-4.45+3.44=19$ miles (near enough). If therefore you remember your own height of eye when standing on the deck of your own ship, it is possible to obtain the distance of a dipping light by merely taking the geographical range and adding or subtracting a remembered correction which will be zero if your height of eye is 15 feet. Thus, if your height of eye is 9 feet (horizon distance 3·44 m) the correction to be remembered is (near enough) minus 1 mile (4·45—3·44): while if your height of eye is 19 feet (horizon distance 5·00 m) the correction to be remembered is (near enough) plus half a mile (5·00—3·44).

In Admiralty charts made or corrected before 1971 the " visibility " charted is the geographical range and therefore the distance of a dipping light can be directly obtained from the charted visibility by merely applying the correction for your own height of eye. Thus if, on a pre-1971 chart, the charted visibility is 15 miles for a light which is seen to dip on the horizon from a height of 9 feet, its distance is (near enough) 14 miles (15—4·45+3·44).

The practice of charting geographical range has, however, been discarded on later charts (including metric charts) and nominal range is now charted, although, of course, geographical range is obtainable from other sources, e.g. Light Lists.

If you do not know the geographical range but only the nominal range, e.g. from a modern chart, the above convenient trick of applying a remembered correction will not work, but the distance away is still easily calculated by adding the horizon distance for the height of the light (from the chart or the Light List, corrected, if necessary, for any fall of tide below High Water Springs in the case of a shore light) to the horizon distance for your own height of eye. Thus, if the height of a light is 120 feet, its horizon distance is 12·6 miles (see Appendix 6) and, if this light is seen to dip on the horizon from a height of 9 feet (horizon distance 3·44 m), its distance from the observer is 12·6+3·44=16 miles (near enough).

" **Arming** " **the Lead.** Much valuable assistance, especially in thick weather, can often be obtained by taking a sample of the sea bottom and comparing it with the chart. Although it is obvious that, at best, only a very approximate position can be obtained in this way, and then only in favourable circumstances, information as to the nature of the sea bottom, taken in conjunction with frequent soundings and a carefully kept dead reckoning, is often most useful. For example, off the south coast of the Isle of Wight the bottom in about 10 fathoms is mainly gravel and shingle at first, becoming principally rock round St. Catherine's Point to beyond Ventnor, and then giving place to a considerable patch of sand and mud in Sandown Bay. A ship in fog, coasting carefully eastwards by lead and log about and along the 10-fathoms line, would receive valuable confirmation of her position by sea-bottom samples, and would be assisted thereby in finding a good anchorage out of the way of traffic, in Sandown Bay. Sea-bottom samples are obtained by filling the hollow in the base of the lead with tallow or heavy grease (this is known as " ARMING THE LEAD "), so that a sample will stick to the tallow or grease and be brought up for examination.

Running a Line of Soundings. An approximate position —sometimes, indeed, a fairly close position—can often be obtained by the method called RUNNING A LINE OF SOUNDINGS. This consists in steering a predetermined course as accurately as possible over the ground, taking regular soundings along the course, reducing them to chart datum so as to be comparable to the soundings on the chart (as explained in Chapters III and IV : " Reduction to soundings " and " Rise and

Fall Table ''), plotting the run and soundings to the scale of the chart on a piece of tracing-paper or celluloid, and then moving

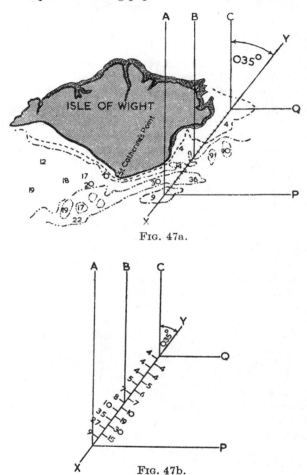

FIG. 47a.

FIG. 47b.

the paper or celluloid about on the chart until, with the plotted run parallel to the course made good, the plotted soundings

fit those marked on the chart.   An example of running a line
of soundings is illustrated in Fig. 47a, which is a simplified
version of the south coastal area of the Isle of Wight.   Suppose
a ship in fog, knowing herself to be somewhere in the neighbourhood of St. Catherine's Point and making good a course
of 035° true over the ground, takes soundings every $\frac{1}{2}$ mile,
obtaining the depths (reduced to soundings) of 9, 15, 27, 30,
35, 19, 10, 10, 8, 7, 7, 6, 5, 5, 4, 4, 4, 4, 4 fathoms over a distance
of 9 miles.   She would know at once that she was not to the
W of St. Catherine's, for nowhere there does a course of 035°
give soundings which increase from under 10 fathoms to over
30 fathoms and then decrease again to 10 fathoms all in a
short distance of under 4 miles.   Her position can be found—
in the present case to a fair degree of accuracy—by drawing
a line XY on a piece of tracing-paper and marking it at every
$\frac{1}{2}$ mile to the scale of the chart.   Opposite each mark is
written the reduced sounding, as shown in Fig. 47b.   It is
convenient to draw a few lines, such as A, B, C, at 035° (the
true course) to the line XY, and one or two other lines such
as P, Q, at right angles to A, B, and C.   The tracing-paper is
then placed over the chart and moved about thereon, keeping
the line XY always at 035° with the aid of the lines A, B, C,
and P, Q, by maintaining the former lines parallel to a meridian
and the latter parallel to a parallel of latitude.   If the soundings have been correctly taken and reduced, some position
(see Fig. 47a) will be found in which the soundings written
on the tracing-paper correspond with the chart soundings immediately beneath them, and this position gives the track the
ship has been following.   The matt side of a Douglas
protractor is most convenient to use for this purpose in place of
tracing-paper, and when so used the lines A, B, C, P, Q may
be omitted, the existing ruled lines on the protractor being
employed instead to orient the course line XY.

   Caution.   When running a line of soundings it is important:
(a) to reduce the casts of the lead accurately to soundings;
(b) to take into account any material current or tidal stream
in estimating the course and distance made good over the
ground; and (c) *to examine the chart most carefully to ascertain*

that the line of soundings will not " fit " in more than one place.
In practice it often pays, in fog, deliberately to select a
temporary course which is both safe and will give an easily
identifiable line of soundings if the ship is where she is thought
to be.

Liners and Packets. A thoroughly reliable " position line "
can often be obtained by observing a liner or packet on her
regular passage. Such ships adhere very closely indeed to
their routes, and the information to be gleaned, for example,
by observing the Dover–Calais packet on passage, is by no
means to be disdained. Be sure, however, that you recognise
the ship and know her passage. Do not assume that any
ship you see is going your way or is even in your channel,
while, as respects other little ships, small coasters, and the
like, there is (or should be) no reason to assume that her
navigation is any more competent than your own.

Fog Navigation. Apart from radio aids, the lead or echo
sounder is the navigator's only real assistant in fog, and repeated
soundings should be taken to check the position. It is sometimes possible to receive warning of a cliffy coast by hearing the
echo of your own horn or syren, and it is perhaps worth remembering that 9/10ths of the interval, in seconds, between a noise
and its echo is (very nearly) equal to the distance in cables of the
object reflecting the echo. *It is strongly recommended, however,
to pay attention to distance measurement by echo only when such
measurements warn you that you are nearing danger—never when
they indicate you are safe.* The trouble is that you are never sure
what is reflecting the echo. It is quite easy to approach
dangerously close to a broken, shelving part of a cliff and obtain
no echo from it, while a good firm echo comes back to you from a
large building or hill inshore, or even from a higher, more vertical
part of the same cliff well to one side of you. Never be
surprised if you do not hear a buoy's fog signal in fog; it does
not mean that you are not near it. Apart from the curious
tricks fog plays with the propagation of sound—it is not
uncommon to hear a light vessel at a mile and lose it at a
quarter of a mile—the fog-horns, bells, and so on fitted to
many buoys are actuated by the movements of the buoy in

the sea. If, therefore, the fog is accompanied by a flat or nearly flat calm, as is a common meteorological combination, many a buoy will not be heard because there is insufficient movement to work the fog-signal apparatus fitted to it.   If you are in a position where you think you should hear a fog signal and do not do so, stop the ship, order silence, and listen carefully, at first at low level and then from some elevated position, as in the rigging. Sounds which are inaudible at sea-level can sometimes be heard clearly from 10 or 15 feet up.

Judgment of Direction of Sound in Fog.   Judgment of the direction of a sound can often be greatly assisted by cupping the hands behind the ears and turning the head from side to side. It will usually be found possible to judge, from the change in sound thus produced, when you are facing the source of sound. It is also a good trick, if a megaphone is carried, to close one ear with the finger and listen through the megaphone with the other.   A more or less well defined maximum of sound will usually be heard when the megaphone is pointed towards the source of sound.

Safety in Fog.   Undoubtedly the safest action when caught by fog is to get out of steamers' tracks as soon as possible. If coasting off a shelving shore, free of rocks and similar dangers, it is, in general, a good plan to calculate the height of tide at the time and then close the shore by the lead and anchor in a depth which is just sufficient to float you safely at dead low water.   Having regard to the shallow draught of most little ships, such an anchorage is unlikely to be disturbed.   At the first signs of fog take a good look round the horizon and note the positions, and, so far as you can, the courses, of any ships not actually receding from you.   Then make out of the way inshore at a reasonable speed.   In many if not most cases, a " reasonable speed " in a little ship means full speed.   If your maximum speed is 5 or 6 knots it is recommended to travel at that speed until the lead tells you that you are in the safety of shallows, or until or unless you hear another vessel forward of your beam.   Remember that it is overwhelmingly probable that you will hear or see a steamer well before she hears or sees you (unless she has radar), and that, in the last resort, the avoidance of a collision with a bigger ship will probably depend upon your own mobility. In general, if you decide to continue a coastal passage in fog, it is best, if ordinary considerations of safe navigation allow, to continue by creeping along shore as close as possible. Above all, make up your mind whether you will go inshore or go well out, and *don't carry out your decision half-heartedly*. Go right in or right out; do not coast in fog only sufficiently far out to lose the land without being clear, and not sufficiently far in to be in " little ship shallows."

CHAPTER XV

NAVIGATION AIDS AND BUOYAGE SYSTEMS

Navigation aids are provided by the various National Authorities almost everywhere in the world to mark principal coastal features, shoals, and other off-lying dangers, fairways, and so on. The most important are lights, including lighthouses, light vessels and floats, lit beacons and buoys; unlit beacons and buoys; radio beacons; leading marks; and fog signals of various kinds. The positions and details of the various navigation aids are given on the charts to an extent of detail dependent on the scale; the larger the scale the more the detail. On large-scale charts the information is practically complete; on smaller scale coastal charts only the principal lights and fog signals, such as would be required to assist in approaching land, are given. On ocean charts only lights visible for 15 miles or more are usually marked, and then the only usual particulars are the character (whether fixed, flashing, occulting, and so on) and colour. In general the omission of detail of lights as the scale gets smaller follows a definite system, details being *omitted* in the following order : elevation, period, number in group, and, the last to be omitted, visibility. *It is therefore most important when navigating in narrow waters (as the little ship usually does) to use the largest scale chart.*

Identification of Lights. Lights are distinguished from one another by *character, period,* and *colour.* By *character* is meant the nature of the " signal " the light gives; whether it is fixed, flashing, occulting, or alternating. By *period* is meant the time interval at which the " signal " (if other than a fixed light) repeats itself. A *fixed* light is one that remains steadily and continuously on. Fixed white lights are very little used as major navigation aids, for the obvious reason that they are liable to confusion with other lights. A *quick flashing* light is one that flashes at approximately 60 flashes per minute. A *very quick flashing* light flashes at approximately 120 flashes per minute. Such flashing may be *interrupted* or *group interrupted*. A *flashing* light is one that gives flashes each separated from the next by an interval of darkness a good deal longer than the flash. The flashes may be single or in groups of two, three, or more. Such a light is said to be *group flashing*. An *occulting* light is one that is extinguished for short periods, each period of extinction being separated from the next by a considerably longer interval of light. An occulting light may thus be regarded as a sort of opposite to a flashing one, the functions of light and darkness being reversed in the two cases. The occultations (extinctions) may be single or in groups of two, three, or more. Such a light is said to be *group occulting*. An *alternating* light is one that changes colour at regular intervals. Unless otherwise stated on the chart or in the light list, a light is assumed to be white. These different *characters* may be used in combination : thus a light which is *fixed and flashing* exhibits a steady, continuous light with one or more flashes of greatly increased brilliance at regular intervals.

The *period* of a light is as important to identification as the character, and is, as already stated, the interval at which the light repeats its characterising " signal." Thus a light which is " Gp. Occ. (2) ev. 8 sec." occults, *i.e.* goes out, twice in succession at the stated interval of 8 seconds between the first of each pair of extinctions and the first of the next pair. When the character or " signal " of a light has been observed, the period should be carefully noted, preferably with the aid of the second hand of a watch. It will be found, however, that with a little practice, seconds up to about half a minute can be reckoned without a watch with sufficient accuracy for period identification, by counting aloud thus : " One, dammit, two, dammit, three, dammit . . ." and so on, speaking the words clearly and with the emphasis that would ordinarily be used by those misguided enough to include them in their vocabulary.

When about to make a landfall by night, always note in advance any major light you should pick up, together with the approximate time you should see it. Indeed, the wise navigator, making anything that could be called a passage, always shapes his course to make a landfall at a major recognisable mark. *The best of all such marks is a major light at night.* If your passage terminates on a coast which is strange to you, it is good practice to time your arrival in the offing before dawn, so that you can fix your position by major lights and then close the land in daylight. *Such a fix is thoroughly reliable : identification of the coast by personal recognition is not.* The author well remembers a case in which a temporary hand, a Manx fisherman born and bred near Douglas, " recognised " as Lynus Point a part of the Welsh mainland seen, in exceptional local dawn visibility, across the Skerries, with results which might have been disastrous had any notice been taken of him.

Arcs of Visibility. Arcs of Colour. Many lights, indeed most shore lights, are not visible from all directions, but are obscured, either by mechanical means provided in the light mechanism itself or by neighbouring land, or both, in certain directions. The arc over which a light is visible is called the ARC OF VISIBILITY, and is defined in the Light Lists or similar publications in terms of bearings—always, unless otherwise stated, true bearings—*given from seaward.* Thus a light described as visible from E (090°) through S (180°) to W (270°) would be visible from a ship so positioned that a bearing, *taken from the ship*, would be between 090° and 270° through 180°. In other words, the light would be visible in the northern half circle *as seen from the lighthouse.* This is illustrated in Fig. 48. Many lights show different colours in different arcs. Such ARCS OF COLOUR, and also arcs of visibility, are often drawn on the chart. The colour seen from the ship gives a reliable indication of the arc in which the ship lies, *but a change from one colour to another should never be relied upon as a position line : a bearing should always be taken for this purpose.* It should be noted also that such arcs of circles drawn round the lights are not intended to indicate the *distances* at which lights can be seen, but solely to indicate arcs of visibility or arcs over which certain colours (or other characteristics) are observable.

Unwatched Lights. The mechanisms of light buoys are,

of course, automatic, and although failures are not common, they occur sometimes. A certain amount of caution is therefore necessary in relying upon buoys which may be temporarily

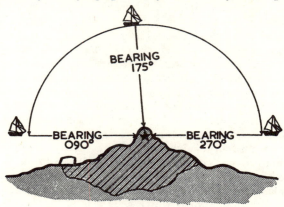

VISIBLE FROM 090° THROUGH 180° TO 270°.

FIG. 48.

out of action or out of position for one reason or another. Do not assume your navigation has gone wrong merely because you fail to find a light buoy which should lie on your course. Check over your working and if you find no error or reasonable probability of error, carry on with your plan. Similar remarks apply to automatic shore lights. Such lights are indicated on older fathom charts by the letter (U) meaning " unwatched " but this letter is obsolescent.

Light Lists, Buoys, etc. Information as to lights is contained in the Admiralty Light Lists, and information as to navigation aids generally is on the charts and to some extent in the pilot books. As regards home waters, however, probably the most conveniently arranged source of information as to navigation aids, from the little ship point of view, is the " Lights, buoys, fog signals, etc." section of *Reed's Nautical Almanac* but yachtsmen with the future intention of going outside the geographical limits of this section of Reed's would be well advised to accustom themselves to using the Admiralty Light Lists.

Buoyage Systems. Buoys are installed in accordance with definite systems that vary from country to country. A few years ago it was not difficult for a navigator even without a chart to get a fairly good idea of the " run " of fairways and the positions and general nature of dangers near his intended track by merely looking at the buoys. Owing, however, to the adoption of new buoyage systems and the gradual replacement of buoys in accordance with one system by buoys in accordance with another, matters are considerably more complex, at any rate temporarily, than they were. At the time of writing, buoys which have been established for years in European waters are being taken up and replaced by others with quite different characteristics and such changes are so frequent that a chart, bought in spring and correctly showing the buoyage of an important channel at the time of purchase, can easily be completely out of date by the following autumn as regards the characteristics of those buoys. Buoyage changes are notified as they occur in Admiralty Notices to Mariners and it is more important than ever for yachtsmen to take these Notices in order to keep their charts up to date.

Side Marking (lateral) and Cardinal. Principles. One or other of two different principles is employed in all the systems. The principle employed in SIDE MARKING or LATERAL systems is that of distinguishing between port and starboard hand buoys in terms of the direction of the main flood stream or of the direction of approach to a harbour, river, or estuary from sea-ward. By this distinction a port hand buoy is one that should be passed to port by a mariner *travelling with the main flood stream, or approaching a harbour or the like from seaward.* Similarly a starboard hand buoy is one that is left to starboard by the mariner *travelling with the main flood stream or approaching a harbour from seaward.*

The principle employed in CARDINAL systems is independent both of the direction of the flood stream and of the direction of approach from seaward, and is based solely on the true bearing of a buoy from the danger it is employed to mark. In this system the danger is regarded as being in the centre of a circle which is divided into four quadrants, namely: a northern quadrant (NW to NE); an eastern quadrant (NE to SE); a southern quadrant (SE to SW); and a western quadrant (SW to NW). The type of buoy employed depends solely on the quadrant in which it lies.

Old British Side Marking Systems. The old BRITISH SIDE MARKING system is described below and illustrated in Fig. 49. It is likely to persist for some time in places.

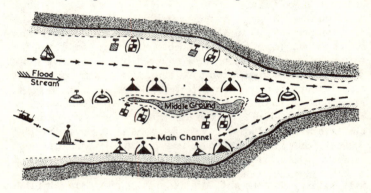

OLD BRITISH SIDE SYSTEM
Fig. 49.

STARBOARD HAND MARKS.

Shape: Conical.

Colour: Black or black and white chequer.

Top-mark (if any): Black cone, point up or black diamond, except at a channel entrance.

Light (if any): White with 1, 3, or 5 flashes.

PORT HAND MARKS.

Shape: Can.

Colour: Red or red and white chequer.

Top-mark (if any): Red can or red T except at a channel entrance.

Light (if any): Red with any number of flashes up to 4 or white with 2, 4 or 6 flashes.

MIDDLE GROUND MARKS.

Shape: Spherical.

Colour: Black and white horizontal bands where main channel is to the left.   Red and white horizontal bands in other cases.

Top-marks (if any):

Red can at outer end⎱
Red T at inner end ⎰ where main channel to right.

Black cone at outer end   ⎱
Black diamond at inner end ⎰ where main channel to left.

Red sphere at outer end   ⎱ where channels
Red St. George's cross at inner end ⎰ equal.

Lights (if any): Distinctive with no colours other than red or white and neither colour nor rhythm such as to lead to uncertainty as to the side the mark should be passed.

MID-CHANNEL OR FAIRWAY MARKS.

Shape: Distinctive, other than cone, can, or sphere.

Colour: Black and white vertical stripes or red and white vertical stripes.

Top-mark (if any): Distinctive other than cone, can, or sphere.

Lights (if any): Distinctive and different from nearby lights or channel side lights.

ISOLATED DANGER MARKS.

Shape: Spherical.

Colour: Wide black and red horizontal bands with a narrow white band between them.

Top-mark (if any): Sphere painted black or red or half black— half red divided horizontally.

Lights (if any): White or red flashing.

LANDFALL MARKS.

Shape: As for channel marking.

Colour: Black and white or red and white vertical stripes.

Lights (if any): Flashing.

WRECK BUOYS

Shape: Starboard hand, conical.
        Port hand, can.
        Either hand, spherical.
Colour: Green with WRECK or W in white.
Lights (if any): Starboard hand, triple flashing green.
                Port hand, double flashing green.
                Either hand, single flashing green.

WRECK MARKING VESSELS

Starboard hand: 3 vertical green lights by night.
               3 vertical green balls or shapes by day.
               3 bell strokes every 30 seconds in fog.
Port hand: 2 vertical green lights by night.
               2 vertical green balls or shapes by day.
               2 bell strokes every 30 seconds in fog.
Either hand: 4 green lights in 2 vertical pairs by night.
               4 green balls or shapes in 2 vertical pairs by day.
               4 bell strokes every 30 seconds in fog.
   Wreck ships are painted green with WRECK in white.

Old Cardinal System. This system, which has been very considerably used in European waters—notably in French (and Algerian) waters but is, at the time of writing, in process of being replaced by a Cardinal system using different buoys, is illustrated in Fig. 50 and described below:

NORTH QUADRANT (NW–NE).

Ordinary buoy: Conical, black with a wide white band and a top-mark consisting of 2 cones, points up, one over the other.

Wreck buoy: None used in this quadrant.

EAST QUADRANT (NE–SE)

Ordinary buoy: Ogival (pointed arch shape) or spar, upper half red, lower half white, with a top-mark consisting of 2 cones, base to base, one over the other.

Wreck buoy : As ordinary buoy but painted green.

SOUTH QUADRANT (SE–SW).

Ordinary buoy : Can, red with a wide white stripe and having a top-mark consisting of 2 cones, points down, one over the other.

Wreck buoy : None used in this quadrant.

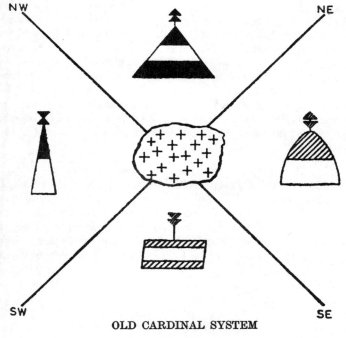

OLD CARDINAL SYSTEM

FIG. 50.

WESTERN QUADRANT (SW–NW).

Ordinary buoy : Spire (thin pointed shape) or spar, upper half black, lower half white, with top-mark consisting of 2 cones, point to point, one over the other.

Wreck buoy : As ordinary buoy but painted green.

I.A.L.A. Buoyage System 'A'. As from April, 1977 a new buoyage system, called I.A.L.A. SYSTEM 'A', is being introduced in British and European waters. It has already been adopted in some places in British waters. It still involves the use of the Lateral or Side Marking principle for channels and the like and the use of the Cardinal principle for small areas of navigational importance, *e.g.* more or less isolated areas of rocks. There are, however, major changes, principally as respects the colours of the lights on lit buoys marking channels and the like (lateral buoys). For such buoys the colours of the lights are chosen in accordance with the idea " red to port: green to starboard," red lights being used for buoys which the mariner should leave to port when travelling with the flood stream or entering harbour, and green lights being used for buoys which he should leave to starboard in these circumstances. *This change involves that green is no longer reserved for wrecks, for which no special characteristics are reserved in this system.*

Fig. 51 illustrates the I.A.L.A. buoyage system 'A' and includes both its Lateral and Cardinal parts. Its principal features are set out below. The arrow head with dots, one open and the other full, is printed in purple on charts to indicate the direction of the flood stream or that of approaching a harbour in order to distinguish between port and starboard in the buoyage system in cases in which this is not obvious.

I.A.L.A. Lateral buoys:

Port Hand.	Shape—	Can, pillar, or spar.
	Colour—	Red.
	Topmark (if any)—	Can.
	Light (if any)—	Red. Any rhythm.
Stbd Hand.	Shape—	Cone, pillar or spar.
	Colour—	Green.
	Topmark (if any)—	Cone, point up.
	Light (if any)—	Green Any rhythm.

I.A.L.A. Cardinal buoys:

| N. Quadrant. | Shape— | Pillar or spar. |
| | Colour— | Black over yellow. |

	Topmark—	Two superimposed black cones, points up.
	Light (if any)	White. Qk. or V. Qk. Fl.
E. Quadrant.	Shape—	Pillar or spar.
	Colour—	Black with yellow band.
	Topmark—	Two superimposed black cones, base to base.
	Light (if any)—	White. Qk. Fl.(3) 10 sec. or V. Qk. Fl.(3) 5 sec.
S. Quadrant.	Shape—	Pillar or spar.
	Colour—	Yellow over black.
	Topmark—	Two superimposed black cones, points down.
	Light (if any)	White. Qk. Fl. (6)+L. Fl. 15 sec. or V. Qk. Fl.(6)+ L. Fl. 10 sec.
W. Quadrant.	Shape—	Pillar or spar.
	Colour—	Yellow with black band.
	Topmark	Two superimposed black cones, point to point.
	Light (if any)	White. Qk. Fl.(9) 15 sec. or V. Qk. Fl.(9) 10 sec.

I.A.L.A. other buoys:

Safe water (Landfall etc.)	Shape—	Sphere, pillar, or spar.
	Colour—	Red and white vertical stripes.
	Topmark (if any)—	Red Sphere.
	Light (if any)—	White. L. Fl., Occ., or Iso.
Isolated danger.	Shape—	Pillar or spar.
	Colour—	Black with one or more red bands.
	Topmark—	Two superimposed black spheres.
	Light (if any)—	White. Gp. Fl.(2)

LATERAL

Port   **Starboard**

Buoyage Direction

CARDINAL

OTHER MARKS

Fairway or Landfall   **Isolated Danger**

I A L A System 'A'

FIG. 51.

The buoyage information given in this chapter is in accordance with general standardised practice but variations from this may occasionally be found. A further IALA system—system B— is contemplated but is still (1976) being prepared.

CHAPTER XVI

PILOTAGE

Pilotage, which may for little ship purposes be defined as harbour, estuary, and other navigation very close to land, does not differ essentially from other forms of coastal navigation, such differences as there are being rather of degree than of kind. There are, however, two important practical differences. The first is that pilotage is commonly subject to purely local tidal streams, which are often not given on the chart or in the tidal atlases. The second is that, owing to the closeness of the land, it is possible to steer by eye to a much greater extent than in ordinary coastal navigation. In spite of the apparent simplicity induced by the latter fact, care is as essential in pilotage as in any other form of navigation, and it is probably true that more little ships go aground during pilotage through abandoning proper navigational caution and steering by the unaided eye than through any other single fault.

Pilot Books. Before entering a harbour for the first time, study the harbour plan, if available, and carefully read any information contained in the appropriate pilot book. If the official pilot books are used—and they are strongly recommended on the ground of completeness—*open any supplement there may be to ensure that there has been no change since the book was printed*. Supplements, which are issued free to the holders of the books, can be most conveniently kept inside the front covers of the books to which they relate. Though the official pilot books contain a great deal more information than the little ship usually wants, in practically every case they give some items she cannot afford not to know, and too much is better than too little. Items to which particular attention should be paid are: (1) dangers; (2) directions for

171

approaching and entering; (3) local tidal streams, usually given with reference to the time of high water at a nearby standard port; (4) navigation aids and leading marks, whether man-made or natural; and (5) the form and meaning of signals which may be exhibited (for example, tide indicators or signals controlling entry into and exit from the harbour) and the places where they are exhibited. In addition they are liberally illustrated with photographs which greatly facilitate recognition. In general, by a careful reading of the appropriate book and a study of the appropriate harbour plan, the navigator can acquire a good advance mental picture before entering. In one respect only are the official pilot books occasionally misleading to the little ship, and that is as regards recommended outside anchorages. In general these are chosen with the big ship in mind, and are not infrequently uncomfortable and sometimes even unsafe for a little ship. Before deciding on an anchorage from the pilot book, therefore, plot it on the chart and use your own judgment as to whether it is suitable for you.

Plan for Entering Harbour. Do not regard the navigational work of a passage as finished when the entrance to the final harbour is seen, but plan out your courses through the entrance and in the harbour itself if it is new to you. This is especially advisable if entering at night. Take your largest available scale chart and draw out your intended tracks on it, however short they may be, and mark the compass courses along them. Then examine the chart for leading marks, lights and so forth, drawing out any bearing lines which may be useful to you, for example to act as safety lines clearing sandbanks or other obstructions. A large harbour liberally bestrewn with sandbanks may appear when you enter to be much more complex than expected, and it is surprisingly easy to be " lost " in such a harbour a couple of minutes after entering. *Do not rely upon finding your way up a lengthy harbour fairway by recognising the successive buoys marking its edges, but if possible pick out major marks which will provide bearing lines running up the channels.* Almost always such marks will be found available, but in any event draw out the successive compass

courses. Only in this way can the ever-present risk of steering
on the wrong buoy be minimised.

An example of a prepared plan for Poole is given with

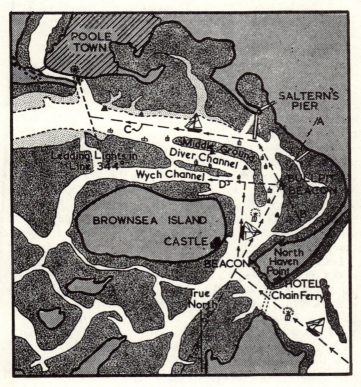

Fig. 52.

reference to the simplified sketch shown in Fig. 52. This
harbour is large and consists mostly of sandbanks with quite
a number of channels. From Fig. 52, it will be seen how little
preparation is required to resolve such a complex harbour into
a very simple navigating proposition. On entering via the
Swash Channel a beacon will be seen on the edge of the mud flat

off North Haven Point.   Bullpit Beacon is situated on the east side of the main channel near the middle of the bend in it. Accordingly, if the bearing line A (028° true) is drawn on the chart it is a simple matter, after passing the beacon at North Haven, to steer by compass (028° corrected for variation and deviation) straight up the middle of the main channel, when the channel marking buoys will be easily found.   Even in thick weather in daylight, when perhaps Bullpit Beacon could not be seen from inside the entrance, a ship could proceed safely by keeping North Haven beacon astern bearing 208° (028° reversed) until Bullpit Beacon or the preceding channel buoys could be picked up.   After passing Bullpit, a back bearing thereon (bearing line B) would enable the end of Saltern's Pier, or the nearby buoy, to be picked out, after which it is easy to alter course on to the last leg C before proceeding right up to Poole.   Similarly, if bound into the Wych Channel, a ship passing along the west side of the middle ground, could find the entrance to Wych Channel with certainty by holding her course until Bullpit Beacon bore the correct amount south of east as indicated by bearing line D, and then using this bearing line as a back bearing.

Back Bearings in Pilotage. Back bearings are much neglected by little ships, but are nevertheless invaluable for them, especially in thick weather. In general, especially in mist, a mark which has been passed can be kept in sight at a distance considerably greater than that at which the same mark could be picked up in the same conditions of visibility. Accordingly, if steering a course from one mark to another, it is an excellent plan to keep accurately to the chosen track by repeated back bearings on the mark you have passed until the next mark is picked up and identified, or until the first mark is lost. In this way much more certain navigation is achieved. The result, as compared to ignoring a mark once you have passed it, is, from the navigating point of view, as though the distance between the marks was more than halved.

" Temporary " Leading Marks. Once a mark has been picked up on the correct bearing, much work with the compass

and on the chart can be saved by observing some fixed object—
it does not in the least matter what—which is in transit
with the mark on that bearing. In harbours and close waters
generally it will usually be found that some object or other—
the end of a house, a lamp-standard, a hole in a hedge, a
break in a wall—is in line with the mark when on the correct
bearing. If there be such an object, note it, and thereafter
steer by keeping the object in line with the mark. This is
considerably easier to do and less liable to error than steering
by compass, and, moreover, the effect of any cross stream is
automatically countered.

Steering on Transits. The rule for steering to keep in line
two objects which are ahead of you is extremely simple:
follow the nearer object. If the nearer object appears to move
to the right of the further one steer more to the right; if it
appears to move to the left steer more to the left. Remember
that transits on objects aft of you are just as useful—often
more useful—than transits on objects ahead, and an accurate
track can be kept by getting the helmsman to face aft and steer
so as to keep a mark you have passed in line with some chosen
object behind it. In this case, of course, the above steering
rule is reversed; if the nearer object appears to move to the
right (as seen by a helmsman facing aft) course should be
altered to port.

Observing Tidal Streams. It is very important to observe
continuously and closely, any cross streams that may affect
you when entering a harbour, for such streams may vary in
strength rapidly over very short distances and may, indeed,
even reverse in direction. To quote but one well-known, if
somewhat extreme, example, when the tidal stream off the
western entrance of Dover harbour is setting strongly to
the eastward at about 2 hours before H.W., the local stream
at the entrance itself is setting hard to the westward, so
that a ship heading north into the harbour experiences
a complete reversal of a strong cross stream in a very short
distance. If the effect of the stream is continuously watched
the course can be continuously varied to counter the stream
as soon as it is felt. If this is not done the ship may be carried

down a long way off her safe track before there is any realisation of what is happening, with results which are nearly always inconvenient and may in some cases be dangerous. When approaching a harbour, lay off the safe track on the chart. Take off the corrected compass course which corresponds to it, and as soon as the entrance can be clearly discerned, head the ship in by compass. Then, while accurately holding the compass course, pick out two objects which can be seen through the entrance and are in transit on that course. Thereafter steer to keep the objects in transit as described in the last paragraph. If this be done any cross stream will be automatically and continuously countered. Furthermore, the direction of the stream can be observed by noticing what compass course is actually being steered while the transit is maintained, while, in addition, an estimate of the strength of the stream can be made by noticing *how much* the steered compass course differs from the course as taken from the chart. This is illustrated in Fig. 53 for the case of a ship entering Calais, where, at springs, a cross stream reaching nearly 3 knots is experienced. From the harbour plan it can be seen that the bearing line A, about 140° true, to the conspicuous lighthouse among the buildings behind the port, passes through the middle of the entrance between the pier heads. Accordingly, in the absence of any stream, a ship entering Calais by keeping the lighthouse in the middle of the entrance would be steering 140° true. If, however, the stream was setting ENE, the course steered while maintaining the lighthouse in transit with the middle of the entrance would be more than 140° true—perhaps 170°. Similarly, with a WSW stream the course steered would be less than 140°—perhaps 110°. Thus, once correctly on the transit, the compass tells you in which direction the stream is setting and whether it is strong or not, for the stronger the cross stream the more will the compass reading differ from the " transit " course corresponding to that taken from the chart.

Use of Hand Bearing Compass to Maintain Track. If, as sometimes happens, you are unable to find a good local transit to steer by, use the hand bearing compass to take frequent checks of the bearing of the mark you are approaching. *Do not merely steer a fixed compass course, and, above all,*

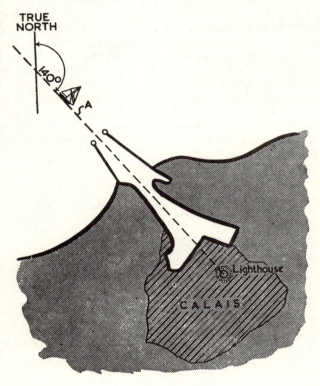

FIG. 53.

do not merely steer on the mark. A fixed compass course will be wrong if your allowance for cross tide is wrong, as it may well be, while merely steering on the mark will cause you to follow over the ground a curved track which is downstream of your intended straight track. Begin by steering a compass course which *you think* contains sufficient allowance to counter the cross stream. Then, while approaching the mark, take repeated bearings of it with the hand bearing compass. If your allowance for stream is right the bearing will remain constant at the correct value. If the bearings change you have allowed either too much or too little and your course should be corrected accordingly. The rule for such correction is : *follow the changes in the hand bearing compass readings.* If the bearing changes to starboard, steer more to starboard, if to port steer more to port. Thus, if endeavouring to keep the lighthouse in Fig. 53 bearing 140° true (150° magnetic, say), the ship should be headed more to starboard if the magnetic bearing becomes, say, 153°, for this is a change to starboard from 150° magnetic. Similarly, if the bearing becomes 147°, say, the ship should be headed more to port.

CHAPTER XVII

THE LOG BOOK

So far this book has dealt with coastal navigation from the aspects of planning what is to be done, doing it, and observing the results. There still remains one more aspect, which is just as important as the others, namely, recording what has been done; in other words, keeping the log book. There are innumerable forms of log books recommended for little ship use, and in this matter there are nearly as many different tastes as there are little ship masters. Some people like to use one or other of the ready ruled and printed books which can be purchased from the yacht supply establishments, but probably most navigators will prefer to develop their own form of record best suited to their own practices and ship.

Requirements of the Log Book. It is strongly recommended that, whatever form of log book is adopted, it should fully satisfy at least the following four requirements. First, it should record all courses and distances of the ship and all estimated tidal streams and leeway in such manner that the ship's estimated position can be readily and quickly worked out at any time; secondly, it should record all fixes and position lines with the manner in which they were obtained; thirdly, it should record barometer, wind, sea, and other weather factors with as much detail as the meteorological knowledge of the navigator will allow him to use to advantage; and, fourthly, *the manner and detail in which the first two of these records is made should be such as to allow the navigator readily to check back on any previous calculation or plot to spot any error he may have made*. It is also desirable, in the author's opinion, that the log book record should be sufficiently detailed to allow all position lines, current triangles, and other " working " to be rubbed off the chart as soon as the corresponding log book entries have been made.

Time. There are diverse opinions about the time which should be kept aboard, but it is strongly recommended that whatever time is adopted for the ship's clock should be used for entries in the log book. It is also recommended that, when in home waters, Greenwich Mean Time should be kept aboard. There are, it is true, apparent advantages of convenience in keeping and logging civil time, for example British Summer Time, but it is suggested that these advantages are more concerned with the land than the sea. It may be very distressing to go ashore at a time indicated by the ship's clock only to find that the hostelries have been closed nearly an hour, but it does not endanger the ship; indeed, in some cases rather the contrary. It is likely to be much more serious to be an hour wrong in working out a tide because the ship's clock is keeping British Summer Time and you have forgotten the fact.

Courses. It is recommended to enter, not only all compass courses actually steered, but also the variation and deviation (if any) used in deciding those courses. This information will be found most valuable if you have reason to think that " something has gone wrong " and are checking back in the log book for a possible error. For the same reason, estimated leeway (if any) should be entered, together with any estimated tidal streams.

Bearings. Position Lines and Fixes. Position lines and fixes should be entered in such manner as to allow the accuracy of calculation or plotting to be checked afterwards. Bearings should be entered as taken by the compass, together with the variation and deviation applied and the resultant true bearing as actually plotted. Thus if a bearing of Cap Griz Nez, taken with the ship's compass, was found to be N 80° E, the variation being 10° W and the deviation 7° W, it should be entered in some such way as:

    1120   Cap Griz Nez N 80° E Varn. 10° W Devn. 7° W
       073° true.

This entry contains sufficient detail to allow the navigator to discover, on a subsequent check, that he has made an arithmetical error of 10°. Sextant angles should be entered as read on the instrument, together with any index error employed, and in the case of a vertical sextant angle, the calculated distance of the object observed. Details of this sort are probably most conveniently entered in a " Remarks " column.

Frequency of Entries. Although most ready printed and ruled books provide for entries every hour, this is usually not necessary, and it is probably better to leave the time column, like the others, to be filled in when required. Every new course, with its details, should be entered when it takes place, and, similarly, any fixes or position lines obtained and any big changes of wind, sea, or weather should be logged at their own times. It is a good plan to enter the reading of the ship's log whenever any other entry is made, and certainly when any course alteration is made. As regards regular entries, it is recommended to take readings of the log, the barometer, the wind, sea, and weather every three hours. In practice, in ordinary stable conditions, this will be found ample for little ships. Incidentally, it is a good plan to enter in the log book those parts of wireless weather forecasts which concern you.

Working up the Position from the Log Book. As a rule, in coasting work, the majority of the ship's positions entered in the log book will be at odd times as obtained by cross bearings and other fixes. If, however, there are long periods in which such fixes are not obtained, it is a wise precaution to work up the ship's position reasonably often from the courses and distances sailed, the tidal streams experienced, and so on. This may be done either by plotting on the chart or by the method to be described in the next chapter. The result should be, of course, entered in the log book (say in the " Remarks " column) as an estimated or D.R. position. In settled good weather and in waters clear of sandbanks or other dangers to navigation it is probably sufficient to work up the position every six hours, starting from the last reliable " fix " or observed position. In other conditions this should be done at more frequent intervals, say every three hours.

Keeping the Track on the Chart. Most navigators will find it convenient to keep the ship's track on the chart as well as in the log book, but it is wise not to " mess up " the chart with a lot of pencilled working lines. Many problems have, of course, to be worked out on the chart, but when the answers have been obtained and the log book entered up, such working lines should be rubbed out and only the observed position lines, or fixes or D.R. positions, left, with the time against it in each case. A position line is best shown as a broken line on the chart with the time written against its end; a fix or D.R. position is best shown as a small cross in a circle with the time written beneath it and the letters D.R. if it is only a worked up position as distinct from a fix. The ordinary method of working up the position graphically on the chart by simply drawing ship and tidal stream movements thereon is the most generally used in coastal work, but there is another method, much neglected by little ships, which can be used to supplement it and which, in some circumstances, offers great advantages. Indeed, it is sometimes the only really practical way.

The Traverse Table. This method is by means of the TRAVERSE TABLE. On a small-scale chart, such as would be in use on a long passage, a day's run in a little ship occupies a very small space, with the result that, with the graphical method, quite small errors of drawing involve relatively large errors in position. This is especially true if, by reason of foul and changing winds, the day's run includes a considerable number of course alterations and probably also a number of different tidal streams. In such a case, to attempt to work up the ship's position by a series of more or less tiny current triangles, is to invite serious error. Again, even when working on a large-scale chart, the graphical method may present considerable practical difficulties in bad weather conditions. It may be no easy matter to do the chart-work involved with the requisite accuracy in the ill-lit cabin of a little ship, jumping about in a bad sea at night. In such circumstances a method which substitutes calculation in a rough notebook for accurate drawing with the parallel rule on a chart has much to commend it. The manner in which this may be done is explained in the next chapter.

CHAPTER XVIII

THE TRAVERSE TABLE

Diff. Lat. No matter what course a ship makes good over the earth's surface, her movement can be resolved into two components, namely, a movement N or S and a movement E or W. If a ship makes good a course exactly E or W she obviously remains always in the same latitude, but changes her longitude. Similarly if she makes good a course exactly N or S she remains in the same longitude, but changes her latitude. On any other course she changes both latitude and longitude. Consider first the case in which the course made good is N or S. The ship is then sailing along a meridian. Since, by definition, a mile along a meridian is a minute of latitude, the distance made good in miles N or S gives directly the change in latitude. Thus, for example, if a ship, starting from a position 49° 40′ N, 7° 10′ W makes good 50 miles northward, her final position will be 49° 40′+50′ N: 7° 10′ W= 50° 30′ N, 7° 10′ W. In other words she has changed her latitude by 50′. This is known as the DIFFERENCE OF LATITUDE—usually written DIFF. LAT.

Departure and D. Long. Now consider the case of a ship making good a course E or W. The ship is then sailing along a parallel of latitude. Her latitude will remain unchanged, but her longitude will not. *The change in longitude in minutes will not, however, be the same as the number of miles made good E or W*, because, as we have already seen in Chapter II, a mile along a parallel is equal to a minute of longitude only on the Equator. As we get nearer and nearer to a Pole a mile along a parallel becomes bigger and bigger in terms of minutes of longitude. Refer again to Fig. 7 of Chapter II. From this figure it will be obvious that a given distance travelled along the parallel PX will cover a larger angle—in other words involve a larger change of longitude—than the same distance along the Equator. It will also be obvious that, if we know the latitude of the parallel along which we are travelling, we can measure or calculate the change in longitude equivalent to a given number of miles " easting " or " westing." The number of miles E or W is called the DEPARTURE; usually written DEP. In practice the transformation of Dep. into DIFFERENCE OF LONGITUDE (D. LONG.) for any latitude is done without calculation or measurement by simple inspection of that section of the Traverse Table headed " Departure into D. Longitude," where the problem is already worked out. The way to use this section of the table will be described later.

Course and Distance. Now consider the case of a ship following a course such that she changes both her latitude and her longitude. Thus, in Fig. 54, suppose the ship starts from A and makes good a distance AB in a direction N 45° E to B. If we regard the portion of the earth's surface considered as flat—and, for a distance such as that which would be traversed by a little ship in a day or two the error introduced by this assumption is negligibly small—ABC is a plane right-angled triangle, and the result is the same as if the ship had gone N from A to C and then E from C to B. In other words, the ship in going from A to B has made a Diff. Lat. AC and a Dep. (NOT a D. Long.) of CB. Since, in the case illustrated in Fig. 54 the angle CAB is 45°, the Diff. Lat. and the Dep. are equal; manifestly if the angle had been more than 45° the Diff. Lat. would have been smaller and the Dep. larger for the same distance AB. Clearly if we know the distance AB and the angle CAB we can calculate or measure the Diff. Lat. and the Dep., but in practice again, calculation or measurement is unnecessary because the problem is already worked out in the Traverse Table, from which the required answers can be found by direct inspection of the appropriate section of the tables. To use this section of the tables we need to know (1) the DISTANCE (AB in FIG. 54), and (2) the COURSE (the angle CAB in FIG. 54).

Make-up of the Traverse Tables. The traverse tables consist of two sections: (1) the main section, by means of which a known distance on a known course can be resolved into Diff. Lat. and Dep.; and (2) the section by which Dep. can be converted into D. Long. The main section, a portion of which is reproduced in Appendix 7, is simply a series of tabulated solutions of right-angled triangles, such as that

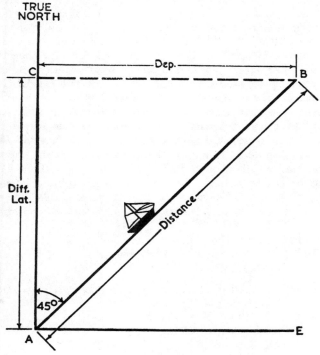

FIG. 54.

shown in Fig. 54, from which, knowing the DISTANCE (AB) and the COURSE (angle CAB), the Diff. Lat. and the Dep. can be taken by inspection. As will be seen from Appendix 7, it consists of a series of sets of vertical columns, each set being headed by a value of distance (the values advancing 1 mile at a time), and comprising a column labelled " Diff. Lat." at

its head and " Dep." at its foot and a column labelled " Dep."
at its head and " Diff. Lat." at its foot. At the side edges of
each page are columns with CO. (course) at the head and foot,
the left-hand column going, by degree intervals, from 1° to
45° and the right-hand column going from 45° to 89°. As is
common in mathematical tables generally, each page can be
read *either downwards and from the left* or *upwards and from
the right*. Thus, suppose a ship makes good a distance of
16 miles N 20° E. The distance is 16 and the course 20°.
This course is found in the left-hand column and therefore
the Diff. Lat. (15·0′) is taken in line with 20° from the column
(for distance 16) *headed* Diff. Lat. The Dep. (5·5′) is similarly
taken from the adjacent column *headed* Dep. Had the same
distance been travelled on a course N 70° E, the Diff. Lat.
would have been 5·5′ and the Dep. 15·0′, because course 70°
is in the extreme right-hand column and therefore the Diff.
Lat. (5·5′) must be taken, in line with 70°, from the column
(for distance 16) labelled Diff. Lat. *at its foot* and the Dep.
must be similarly taken from the adjacent column labelled
Dep. *at its foot*. For working the Traverse Table, courses
(all, of course, true) are expressed in quadrantal notation,
thus, N 10° E or N 15° W or S 27° E or S 30° W. Obviously,
if the first letter of the course is N the Diff. Lat. is N; if it is S
the Diff. Lat. is S. Similarly, if the second letter of the course
is E the Dep. is E; if it is W the Dep. is also W.

Example 1. A ship makes good 16 miles on a course 043°
   true. What is the Diff. Lat. and the Dep.?
   043° = N 43° E in quadrantal notation.
   From the tables with Co. 43° ⎱ Diff. Lat. is 11·7′ N.
      and distance 16   ⎰ Dep. is 10·9′ E.

Example 2. A ship makes good 14 miles on a course 256°
   true. What is the Diff. Lat. and the Dep.?
   256° = S 76° W in quadrantal notation.
   From the tables with Co. 76° ⎱ Diff. Lat. is 3·4′ S.
      and distance 14   ⎰ Dep. is 13·6′ W.

Example 3. A ship makes good 9 miles on a course 350°
   true. What is the Diff. Lat. and the Dep.?

350° = N 10° W in quadrantal notation.

From the tables with Co. 10° ⎱ Diff. Lat. is 8·9' N.
and distance 9   ⎰ Dep. is 1·6' W.

Series of Courses and Distances. A whole series of ship's movements, *whether due to the ship herself or to a tidal stream under her*, can be dealt with in this way and the resultant values of Diff. Lat. added algebraically, *i.e.* with due regard to whether they are N or S, the resultant values of Dep. being similarly added algebraically. Thus, suppose the courses and distances given in Examples 1 and 2 above were courses and distances traversed by a ship through the water and, while she was doing this, she was moved bodily by a tidal stream as in Example 3—namely a tidal stream which set her 9 miles in a direction 350°. Then the total Diff. Lat. and Dep. due to the two " ship " courses and the " stream " course could be found by algebraic addition as follows :

" Ship " : ⎰ 16 miles 043°=Diff. Lat. 11·7 N
           ⎱ 14 miles 256°=   Diff. Lat. 3·4 S
" Stream " : 9 miles 350°=Diff. Lat. 8·9 N _____
                         Diff. Lat. 20·6 N   Diff. Lat. 3·4 S
                                  3·4 S
                  Total Diff. Lat. 17·2 N

" Ship " :   ⎰ Dep. 10·9 E
             ⎱   Dep. 13·6 W
" Stream " :   Dep. 1·6 W
             _____   _____
             Dep. 10·9 E   Dep. 15·2 W
                                  10·9 E
                  Total Dep. 4·3 W

If the ship's starting position had been 49° 40' N, 7° 10' W her new latitude would be 17·2' further N, *i.e.* 49° 40' N +17·2'=49° 57·2' N. To find her new longitude we have merely to convert the total Dep. into D. Long. and apply that to her original longitude. This is done by the second section of the tables, a portion of which is reproduced in Appendix 8.

Dep. into D. Long. Middle Latitude. To use this section we must know the Dep. and the average latitude, or MIDDLE LATITUDE as it is called, half-way between the extremes of latitude between which the ship moves. In the above example the ship moves between Latitude 49° 40′ N and Latitude 49° 57·2′ N so her middle latitude is half the sum of these values

$=\dfrac{49°\ 40′+49°\ 57·2′}{2}=49°\ 48·6′$. In practice it is sufficient

to know the middle latitude to the nearest half degree—often only to the nearest degree—so the foregoing calculation is really unnecessary in this particular example, for which the middle latitude could be taken as 50° N. If, however, the latitude had changed by two or three degrees the calculation, roughly done to the nearest half degree, would have been required. Entering the table " Departure into D. Longitude " (Appendix 8) with Dep. 43 (left or right-hand column: they are the same in this table) and Middle Latitude 50 (top of the page) we get D. Long. 6·69 = (near enough) 6·7. Note that we took 43 instead of 4·3 for Dep. and 6·69 instead of 66·9 for D. Long. It is obviously always permissible to move the decimal point in this way if convenient to do so. Since the D. Long. is 6·7′ W and the original longitude is 7° 10′ W the final longitude is 7° 10′ W+6·7′=7° 16·7′ W.
$=7°\ 16·7′$ W.

The practical simplicity of this use of the Traverse Tables will be seen from the fully worked example below and the amount of " finicky " drawing on the chart which is avoided will be apparent.

Example. A yacht, beating into the Western Approaches from the westward, has the following entries in her log book:

17th July, 1977.

0800 G.M.T. Position 50° 23′ N 9° 36′ W. Course 140° true.
                  Log reading 50.

1200   ,,   Course changed to 040°.   Log 66.

1600   ,,   Course 140°.   Log 82.

2000   ,,   Course 040°.   Log 98, wind falling away.

2400   ,,   Course 095°.   Log 110, wind very light.

18th July, 1977.

0400 G.M.T. Becalmed.   Log 119.

0600   ,,   Light W wind.   Course 100°.   Log 119.

Reference to the tidal atlas gives the following average tidal streams :

0800/17	—	1400	280/1½ knots
1400	—	1500	Slack ,,
1500	—	2000	060/2 ,,
2000	—	2200	Slack ,,
2200/17	—	0400/18	260/1½ ,,
0400	—	0600	Slack

What was the position at 0600/18th July?

Explanation of Working.

The ship's own movements were :

from 0800/17	—1200	: 16 miles	(66–50)	on course	140°
,, 1200	—1600	: 16 ,,	(82–66)	,,	040°
,, 1600	—2000	: 16 ,,	(98–82)	,,	140°
,, 2000	+2400	: 12 ,,	(110–98)	,,	040°
,, 2400/17	—0600/18	: 9 ,,	(119–110)	,,	095°

The tidal streams were :

from 0800/17—1400 : 9 miles (6 hours at 1½ k.) in direction 280°.
,, 1500/17—2000 : 10 miles (5 hours at 2 k.) in direction 060°.
,, 2200/17—0400/18 : 9 miles (6 hours at 1½ k.) in direction 260°.

Working :

Courses True	Distances	Diff. Lat. N	S	Dep. E	W	
140°=S 40° E	66–50 =16	—	12·3	10·3	—	⎫
040°=N 40° E	82–66 =16	12·3	—	10·3	—	⎪
140°=S 40° E	98–82 =16	—	12·3	10·3	—	⎬Ship
040°=N 40° E	110–98 =12	9·2	—	7·7	—	⎪
095°=S 85° E	119–110= 9	—	0·8	9·0	—	⎭
280°=N 80° W	6×1½ = 9	1·6	—	—	8·9	⎫
060°=N 60° E	5×2 =10	5·0	—	8·7	—	⎬Tidal
260°=S 80° W	6×1½ = 9	—	1·6	—	8·9	⎭
		28·1	27·0	56·3	17·8	
		27·0		17·8		

Diff. Lat. ‾1·1 N Dep. 38·5 E

Initial Lat. 50 23′ N
Final Lat. ‾50 24·1′ N

Middle Latitude (to nearest half degree) $50\frac{1}{2}°$ N

Dep. 38·5′ E=D. Long 60·5′ E (Appendix 8) =1°   0·5′ E

Initial Long. =9°   36′ W

Final Long. =8° 35·5′ W

Final Position 50° 24·1′ N, 8° 35·5′ W.

Caution.   In making a working table such as that shown above it is a wise practice to fill in the " course " and " distance " columns *and the " blanks " in the Diff. Lat. and Dep. columns* before opening the traverse tables.   This can be done from the " course " entries.   For a course S and E, blanks must obviously be inserted in the N and W columns. This order of procedure will prevent what is a common slip, namely, that of entering figures in the wrong columns.

Many traverse tables are not in the form shown in Appendix 7 but all are alike in principle and use the same terms, so that their use will be obvious from the foregoing.   If, as is sometimes the case, there is no Dep. into d. Long table, enter the traverse table proper with Mid. Lat. as Course and Dep. as Diff. Lat. and take out d. Long. as Distance.

The traverse table takes a little getting used to, but the trouble is well worth while.   For long-passage navigation it is a real necessity, but even for relatively short coastal work it is often a great advantage, especially in bad weather when drawing is difficult.

CHAPTER XIX

RADIO NAVIGATION AIDS:
DIRECTION FINDERS AND CONSOL

Although radio navigation aids are a great help, it must always be remembered that they are mere aids and are capable of large errors if incautiously used.

Radio Direction Finders (DF). The radio aid most often found in little ships is the ROTATABLE AERIAL DF, or its equivalent, the RADIO GONIOMETER DF. The former has a directional aerial which can be rotated until the received signal is of minimum, theoretically zero, strength, and then indicates on a scale the direction of the received transmitter relative to the ship's head. The latter has a fixed directional aerial system, usually consisting of two loops at right angles, which is connected to an instrument, called a GONIOMETER, having a coil, rotation of which serves the same purpose as rotation of the aerial in the former DF. With most little ship DF's it is often difficult to determine the minimum strength position with adequate precision, even when the receiver " gain " is high. It is good practice, after having found the minimum signal position roughly, to swing the rotatable member a little way, first in one direction and then in the other, to find two positions, close to and on opposite sides of the minimum signal position, at which the signal strength is of the same small but discernible value, and to take as correct a scale reading mid-way between the two equal strength readings on the scale.

Quadrantal Error. It should not be overlooked that a DF is liable to QUADRANTAL ERROR. This is analagous to deviation in a magnetic compass. Just as sources of magnetic interference near a compass can produce deviations which are different on different ship headings, so electrically conductive structures (not necessarily of iron) in the neighbourhood of a DF aerial can

191

produce quadrantal errors which are different on different DF scale readings and can easily amount to 10° or more. Such things as stays, wire halliards, funnels and Radar reflectors are common causes of quadrantal error. Usually quadrantal error is least when the transmitter being received is dead ahead or astern, or dead on either beam. The quadrantal error of the same DF may become quite different if it is moved to a different part of the ship. *Therefore a DF should have a fixed installed position and should be calibrated for error when in that position, to obtain a Quadrantal Error Table for subsequent use.* Not to obtain a Quadrantal Error Table for a DF is like neglecting to obtain a Deviation Table for a steering compass. Calibration is quite easy. It is best done under power on a quiet day. Steam within sight of a radio beacon and a few miles from it and take a series of DF bearings and simultaneous careful hand bearing compass readings of it on a series of different ship headings, right round the circle, at, say, 10° intervals. Keep the ship in the same position as nearly as you can for all observations. Convert the compass readings into True bearings by applying magnetic Variation. The quadrantal error on any DF scale reading is the difference between the true bearing and the DF bearing, the latter being, of course, the DF scale reading applied to the ship's head, true. After the complete " swing " you can prepare a Quadrantal Error Table with DF scale readings in one column and corrections for error in another. Below is an example of data for one entry in such a table:

Ship's head by compass	096	
Compass deviation	2 E	
Magnetic variation	8 W	
Ship's head, true	096+2—8=090	
DF scale reading	60 to Port	
DF bearing, true	090—60	=030
Hand bearing compass reading	043	
Magnetic variation	8 W	
True bearing	043—8	=035
Quadrantal error correction		—5

The correction is —5 because, to have been correct, the scale reading should have been 55 to Port instead of 60. The entries in the table are " 60 Port " in one column and " —5 " in the other.

If there is a convenient charted position, such as a major buoy, two or three miles from the beacon, it is simpler and more accurate to " swing " with the buoy in transit with the beacon, and far enough from the buoy to ensure it will not itself introduce quadrantal error, and find the differences between the DF bearings and the true bearing taken from the chart.

A number of beacons give a calibration service, some as a routine matter and some by request.

Night Effect: Fading: Refraction. The earth is surrounded, high above its surface, by a radio reflecting layer called the ionosphere. It is a very " woolly " sort of reflector, nothing like a good mirror, and its height is neither constant nor the same everywhere, changing considerably and irregularly, especially around the times of morning and evening twilight. Radio waves from a transmitter can, and often do, reach a ship over two wave paths, one—the so-called Ground Wave path—along the earth's surface, and the other—the so-called Sky Wave path—going obliquely up to the ionosphere whence it is reflected down to the ship. Because these paths are of different lengths, the ground and sky waves do not reach the ship simultaneously and may interfere with each other. If the sky wave is strong—and although it can occur by day it is usually much stronger by night (hence the term NIGHT EFFECT)—the interference may be considerable, blurring the minimum signal position by making it indefinite and, worse still, making it wrong by an unknown amount. *Never trust a DF bearing if the minimum signal position is materially less sharply defined than it is in a normally good observation.*

Variations in the height of the ionosphere will obviously produce variations in the interference between ground and sky waves. Such variations may cause FADING, which is a large and more or less rhythmic variation in received signal strength. Fading can occur at any time but it is usually worst near morning and evening twilight. *Never trust a DF bearing if there is fading, for this is a sure indication of the possibility of a large DF error. Because maximum interference between the ground and sky waves is the rule rather than the exception near twilight times, do not take DF bearings at these times.*

REFRACTION is another common source of DF error which has to be watched. The electrical conductivity of the earth's surface is far from uniform. To take the most important difference, the sea is more conductive than the land and therefore the speed of advance of a radio wave over sea differs from its speed over land. Accordingly, if a radio wave crosses a coast line other than perpendicularly, its direction of advance is changed by refraction just as the direction of a light beam is changed when it passes obliquely from air into glass. Since a DF only reads the direction of incoming radio waves and this will not be the same as that of the received transmitter if the wave path to the ship has a bend in it, refraction may cause very substantial error in a DF bearing—errors of as much as 20° can occur if the path crosses a coast line at a very acute angle. Refraction may also occur if the wave path runs close to a large land mass, such as a mountain, or over high land. If possible, therefore, only take DF bearings on radio beacons which are separated from you by uninterrupted sea. *Never take a DF bearing on a beacon the path from which crosses a coast line at an angle of less than 60° or near a large land mass or over a large extent of high land.*

Half Convergency. The path followed by an unrefracted ground wave is a Great Circle (see Chapter II). Unless the transmitter being received is exactly N or S of you, the Great Circle path is not represented on a Mercator chart by a straight line but by a curved line which joins the straight line at its ends and is on the side of it nearer the more adjacent Pole of the earth. If therefore, having taken a DF bearing, you draw it on a Mercator chart as you would a compass bearing, its direction will be drawn incorrectly (unless the transmitter is N or S) by an angle known as the HALF CONVERGENCY angle (see the angles at X1 and X2 in Figure 10) and the DF bearing should have been corrected by this angle before being drawn on the chart. The correction is always applied *towards the equator.* For little ship navigation the half convergency correction may be regarded as too small to matter, even if the transmitter is due E or W of you, if it is not more than about 50 miles from the ship, and if you restrict yourself to beacons which are not much further away than this, or are nearly N or S of the ship, you need not bother with half convergency correction. For other cases the required correction can be taken by direct inspection from any of the half convergency tables which are to be found in numerous publications, *e.g.* the excellent pocket sized booklet entitled " Traverse and other Tables for Coastal Yachtsmen " compiled by C. A. Rich and published by Kandy Publications.

Consol. There are many good radio navigation aids which transmit signals from which a ship can obtain a position line without having any direction sensitive receiver aboard. CONSOL, however, is the only one which, from considerations of cost and complexity of the equipment required on board, can fairly be regarded as practical for even the smallest yachts. Although the Consol system is quite complex technically, the complexities are all ashore at the transmitting end. The ship-borne receiver could hardly be simpler: it is merely a slightly modified broadcast receiver—in fact a broadcast and Consol receiver are often combined in the same set.

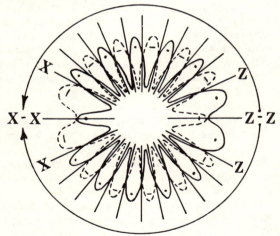

FIG. 55.

Fig. 55 illustrates the Consol principle without going into technical details. The shore transmitter transmits alternately one or other of two patterns of sector-like " beams," those of one pattern (shown in full lines) giving dots and the other (shown in broken lines) giving dashes. The timing of the dots and dashes is such that, on the radial lines where the dot and dash sectors overlap and the two patterns are received at equal strength, a continuous signal is heard. In each operating cycle of the transmitter the top and bottom halves of the diagram of Fig. 55 are caused to rotate in opposite directions until the two equi-signal lines marked X come together on the line X–X, and the equi-signal line Z–Z splits into two lines which move apart until they occupy the two positions marked Z. Wherever you are on the diagram therefore, you will receive a count of dots followed by a count of dashes, or vice versa, with a continuous signal at the change-over. Simply noting whether you start with dots or dashes, and making a count of the number you hear before the continuous signal comes up is all you need to identify your position line (a hyperbolic one) from a number of such lines printed on a Consol chart. These charts are obtainable from Admiralty chart agents and are simply ordinary charts which have been over-printed with hyperbolic position lines in colours appropriated to different Consol stations and marked with dot and dash counts. A fix is obtainable by receiving from two Consol stations in succession, identifying your two position lines by their counts, and noting where they cross.

Consol is a very good off-shore long range aid, quick and easy to use, but its accuracy is not enough for a landfall in thickish weather—Consol fixes may sometimes be in error, especially at night, by as much as 10 miles or so. The accuracy varies round a station, being least on the line X–X–Z–Z in Fig. 55 and best on a line perpendicular thereto. *Choose the stations which will give you the best accuracy having regard to your position.* The European Consol system has four stations—Bushmills (in N. Ireland), Stavanger (in Norway), Ploneis (in France), and Lugo (in Spain)—the arrangement of which is such that you can usually do this. For example Bushmills and Stavanger are the best stations for fixes in the North Sea, the Eastern half of the Irish Sea, and the English Channel east of a line Plymouth/ Cherbourg. The different stations transmit on different long wave frequencies and their operating cycles take different times to go through—*e.g.* 40 seconds for Bushmills and Ploneis and 60 seconds for Stavanger and Lugo. The total number of signals per cycle is the same for all the European stations, namely 60. The operating details of the different stations, with diagrams showing coverage and accuracy, and which can be used to pick the best stations, will be found in a pamphlet C.A.P. 59, " Consol, an aid to Navigation " published by the Stationary Office.

It is usually difficult, when listening to Consol, to determine precisely when the dots (or dashes) merge into a continuous signal. Recommended practice is therefore to count both dots and dashes which can be recognised as such, to add the two counts together, to subtract the sum from 60 (the total number of signals in a cycle), and to add half the difference to each count. Thus, suppose you hear 26 clear dashes preceding a rather indefinite equi-signal, and then 30 clear dots. Since there are 60 signals in a cycle you have lost 60—56 = 4 signals. Add half of this, namely 2, to the dash count and take the " 28 dash " line on the Consol chart as your position line. *Always take several counts when using Consol: if they differ by more than three or four at most, reject the observation—something is wrong— and do not use Consol if you believe yourself to be within about 30 miles of the station you are receiving.*

You can, if you prefer, draw a position line on your own chart instead of using a Consol chart. This can be done with the aid of tables to be found in C.A.P. 59 (supra) and which translate Consol counts into true bearings. If you use these tables remember to apply half convergency correction if necessary. C.A.P. 59 also contains a table giving these corrections. How-ever most little ship navigators will much prefer to use Consol charts—it is so much easier and quicker to do so and they are not expensive.

CHAPTER XX

RADAR

Radar is one of the technical marvels of the age, enabling ships to proceed in fog so thick that, without its aid, they would have anchored or dropped to mere steerage way. This very advantage has, however, considerably increased the risk of collision in fog, and radar, used incautiously, can be a real danger. It was not for nothing that a merchant navy captain, of international standing, read before the Royal Institute of Navigation a paper entitled " Radar Assisted Collisions."

Principles of Radar. A radar consists essentially of a radio transmitter, a continuously rotated aerial providing a directional beam and which is used both for transmission and reception, a receiver, and a display tube. The transmitter generates regularly repeated pulses of radio waves, usually about 1000 pulses of X-band (3 cm.) waves per second, which are transmitted as a beam as the aerial rotates, and which, after reflection by a radio reflecting " target," are received back on the aerial, detected, and used to operate the display tube. Obviously the time interval between the transmission of a pulse and its return after reflection is a measure of the distance away—RANGE—of the target. Small as this interval is—it is only millionths of a second (microseconds)—it can be measured electronically and, because the direction in which the aerial is pointing does not perceptibly change in so short a time, the aerial direction when a pulse is transmitted corresponds with the direction of the target which reflects it. The display tube is, in principle, like the picture tube in a television set. It is a cathode ray tube having a fluorescent screen which glows where it is struck by an electron beam; an " electron gun " for projecting a fine electron beam on to the screen; and a deflecting system which deflects the beam simultaneously in two directions, one radial and the other circular. Each time a pulse is transmitted, a fast radial deflection commences and, at the end of it, and before the next pulse is transmitted, the electron beam is returned, practically instantaneously, to its original undeflected position. While this is going on, the continuous circular deflection of the beam takes place in synchronism with the rotation of the aerial which, to take a typical practical figure, may sweep through 360° of azimuth in 2 seconds. Normally the electron beam in the tube is " suppressed ", so that it is unable to produce a light spot on the screen, but when a reflected radio wave pulse is received it is used momentarily to " brighten up " the beam which accordingly produces on the screen a glowing light spot, the radial position of which indicates target range and the circular position of which indicates target direction. The screen has the property that a light spot produced in this way does not go out immediately the electron beam ceases, but fades away, persisting for an appreciable time. This effect is known as AFTERGLOW and it causes a target to appear on the screen not just as a light spot but as a spot with a TAIL of diminishing brightness—not unlike the tail of a comet— behind it. To facilitate measurement of the Range of a target, the screen is provided with a set of rings, known as RANGE RINGS, centred on the centre of circular rotation, and in order to facilitate measurement of the direction of a target there is provided a BEARING CURSOR in the form of a radial line which can be manually rotated until it passes through a chosen target and its direction read off on a circumferential scale of degrees. Sometimes the Bearing Cursor is a simple radial line but, more conveniently, it may have a central diametrical line with other parallel lines spaced each side of it. In order to provide for convenient watching of short range or long range targets, RANGE CHANGE is provided by a knob control having several positions in each of which the maximum target range which the screen can accommodate is different. For example there might be ranges of 0–3 miles, 0–6 miles, 0–12 miles or other ranges from short to long. In each position of the Range Change control the Range Rings are automatically changed to suit the maximum range which can be displayed in that position, and so also is the radio pulse length—this may be anything from about 0·05 to about 0·75 of a microsecond—longer pulses being used for longer ranges. Finally, once per revolution of the aerial, a radial line, known as the HEADING MARKER, is electronically produced on the screen. In some radars there is a push button control for temporarily eliminating the Heading Marker in order to prevent its obscuring a target.

Relative Motion Head-up Radar. Although big ships often carry much more sophisticated (and expensive) radars, the equipments fitted in the overwhelming majority of little ships are RELATIVE MOTION HEAD-UP RADARS and therefore this chapter is confined to this (the simplest) type of radar. In this type of radar the centre of display represents " own ship "; the top or front of the display represents ship's head; and, if the radar is working correctly, the Heading Marker, which represents the direction of ship's head, is produced each time the aerial is pointing dead ahead. *The bearing of a target, as indicated by the Bearing Cursor, is only its* RELATIVE BEARING, *i.e.* its bearing relative to ship's head. Sometimes the Bearing Cursor scale is calibrated in degrees from 0° (dead ahead) clockwise to 359°: sometimes it is calibrated in degrees increasing from 0° (dead ahead) anti-clockwise to port (Red) and clockwise to starboard (Green). Thus, assuming the former type of scale, if the direction read off for a target is 210° and the ship if heading 300° true, the true target bearing is 300°+210°=510°= (subtracting 360) 150°. With the latter type of scale, add a Green reading to, or subtract a Red reading from, ship's head true to get the true bearing. Thus, with the ship's head and target as before, the scale reading would be Red 150° and the true bearing would be 300°—150°=150°. *It is vital never to forget that only Relative Bearings are given by the Bearing Cursor scale and that a change in the direction in which the ship is steered will produce a corresponding alteration in the scale reading: this is especially important when observing another ship to see if risk of collision (other ship on a constant bearing) exists, for the successive Bearing Cursor scale readings will tell you whether such risk is present or not only if a constant course is steered throughout.*

Clutter. Diffuse radio reflectors, such as heavy rain or showers—RAIN CLUTTER—or sea spray—SEA CLUTTER—can obscure important targets by causing whole areas of glowing on the screen. Sea clutter is seldom seen at ranges exceeding 3 miles and, for obvious reasons, is usually worst to windward. Rain clutter may appear at ranges up to 10 miles or more if the rain is heavy. *If you have a glowing clutter area on your screen, be wary: it may be hiding a ship.* Some radars, too sophisticated to be normal in little ships, have clutter controls which the maker's handbooks will tell you how to use.

Navigating by Radar. Always be cautious about doing this. A radar does not " see " in the same way as your eyes do. Targets vary enormously in their radio reflecting power. Buildings, breakwaters, cliffs, and other things with bare flat vertical surfaces, are excellent reflectors but structures, such as tall chimneys and lighthouses, having well rounded or inclined surfaces, are far less good. A chimney marked " conspic " on the chart may be very far from that on a radar screen. A little ship, especially of wood, is generally a poor target even if she carries a radar reflector (which she should always do in thick weather) and her radar visibility to a big ship's radar is often measurable in cables rather than in miles, especially if there is much sea or rain about. *So keep well clear in thick weather—your radar will probably " see " a big ship long before hers " sees " you.* Be particularly cautious about radar-ranging your distance off shore from the representation of the coast on your screen. You may easily mistake a line of buildings some way inland for a low coastline. In the case of a coastline backed by slowly rising ground the base of which is beyond the radar's horizon and therefore hidden from it, what appears in the radar as the coastline may be a line resembling the coastline in shape but actually a line intersecting the rising ground some way up it and therefore some way inland. Such a line will show up on the screen because the transmitted radio beam has a considerable VERTICAL SPREAD—*i.e.* a taper upwards—usually of about 25°. Again, because of the longer pulses used on longer ranges, weakly reflecting but near targets which would show up on a short range setting may be missed on a longer range setting. Another possible cause of navigational error is

HORIZONTAL BEAM SPREAD (horizontal taper outwards) of the radio beam. This is commonly about 2°. A target of width (dimension in the direction of beam sweep) less than the width of the beam at target range will almost certainly not show up on the screen, and targets such as headlands and small islands which are wide enough to be " picked up " appear on the screen widened at each end by half the beam width at the target range. This effect can cause narrow mouthed inlets to be missed and the coastline to appear continuous on longer ranges. Observation of the following rules will help to make radar navigation coastwise less liable to error, but caution should always be shown:—

1. Check a radar range and bearing " fix " on a coastal target on the bow by taking a radar range of the coastline on the beam and making sure that *both* observations agree with the chart.

2. To get a " fix " by radar ranging, take the ranges of at least three identified targets and plot them on the chart as you would do if the ranges were obtained by vertical sextant angles (See Chapter XIII). *If the three arcs do not cut almost at a point, do not trust the " fix."*

3. Use the shortest range which will put the coastline on your screen and if off-lying dangers make your required distance off shore such that you have to use a long range to do this, switch over to a short range from time to time and check for targets which may have been missed on the longer range.

Heading Marker Error. One of the most dangerous faults which can occur in a radar is for the circular deflection in the display tube to get out of synchronism or alignment with the rotating aerial, so that the latter is not pointing dead ahead when the heading marker is " painted " on the screen. This is HEADING MARKER ERROR and has been the cause of disastrous big ship collisions. Among other things it can make one of two ships meeting end on " see " the other initially fine on one bow and to appear to cross ahead as the two ships close. Check for it in clear weather from time to time as occasion offers by switching on the radar, steaming directly towards a good stationary target, such as a lightship, and, when still a few miles away, use the range which brings the target closest to the edge of the screen and confirm that the heading marker passes correctly through the target and remains there as the approach continues. If you find you have any Heading Marker Error do not trust your radar bearings until the cause of the fault has been found and rectified.

Radar Shadows. Parts of your own ship may obstruct the radio beam as it sweeps round, causing RADAR SHADOWS in which targets may be missed. Common obstructions are spreaders and cross-trees at near aerial height and, in motor vessels, funnels. Get to know the Shadow Sectors of your own ship. Swing *very slowly* through 360° while observing a weakly reflecting stationary target, such as a small moored wooden boat, on the screen, and note and log the sectors, if any, over which the target display disappears or noticeably weakens.

Racons and Ramarks. These are navigation aids fitted with radio transmitters which are " triggered " into action when struck by the radio beam of a ship's radar. RACONS, which are being increasingly used for lightships and lighthouses in British and European waters, produce on the radar screen a strong radial bar or line of dots pointing towards the Racon station. RAMARKS, which have not, at the time of writing, been adopted in British or European waters, but may be so in the future, serve a similar purpose, producing on the screen, at intervals of about a minute, a solid or broken line which points towards the station.

Anti-Collision Radar Plotting. *It is not enough merely to look at the screen of a Relative Motion Head-Up Radar and treat it as though it were a substitute for a pair of eyes, and many collisions have been caused by this dangerous practice.* The importance of radar plotting whenever the time available allows it to be done cannot be over-emphasised. There is an inexpensive Admiralty " Radar Plotting Sheet " (its official number is EXN 30 E) which can be obtained from any Admiralty chart agent. Its regular use in open waters is strongly recommended.

Distant Ship Open Water Situations. These are the situations in which another ship first appears on your screen at such a range as to allow adequate time for plotting. Plotting consists in observing range and relative bearing (the scale reading of the Bearing Cursor) of the other ship at regular intervals—six minute intervals is normal good practice for yachts—and plotting them on a plotting sheet.

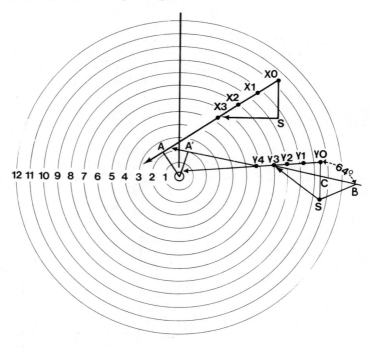

FIG. 56.

Fig. 56 shows a typical distant ship situation. 0 represents the centre of the screen (own ship) and the vertical radial line

represents the Heading Marker. There are shown 12 Range
Rings 1 mile apart and marked 1,2,3 . . . . . 12. Below the
circular part of the figure is a scale of distances which would be
covered in 18 minutes—i.e. in three 6-minute intervals—at
different speeds. Two ships, X and Y, are " seen." One, X,
is about 45° on the starboard bow and the other, Y, is a little
forward of the starboard beam. Both are at a range of about
10½ miles when first seen on the screen. Their relative bearings
and ranges when first observed are noted and their initial
positions, relative to own ship are plotted at X0 and Y0.
Six minutes later they are observed again and the new relative
positions are plotted at X1 and Y1. After another six minutes
they are observed again and their relative positions plotted at
X2 and Y2. A further pair of observations is taken after
another six minutes and added to the plot to give the relative
positions X3 and Y3. If both ships (and, of course, your own)
maintain constant courses and speeds, as they should do in open
waters, X0, X1, X2 and X3 will be equally spaced along a
straight line, as also will Y0, Y1, Y2 and Y3. Continuation of
these straight lines will show the closest approaches of the
respective ships to own ship. In the case of ship X this is
nearly 2½ miles (distance 0A). A closest approach of 2 miles
can be considered safe, so nothing need be done about X
although, naturally, she should be watched in case she alters
for some reason. We can, if we wish, find her course and
speed. Suppose our own course and speed are 060°/10 K.
Draw back from X0 a line X0–S parallel to the Heading Marker
and of a length (taken from the scale in the figure) equal to the
distance we travel in 18 minutes (three 6-minute intervals) at
10 K. Join S to X3. The length S–X3 represents the speed of
X and its direction represents her course relative to our own.
As will be seen, her speed (from the scale) is 15 K and her
relative course is 90° anti-clockwise of ours. Since we are
steaming 060° her course and speed are 060°—90°/15 K=
330°/15 K.

Returning now to ship Y, prolongation of the line Y0—Y1—
Y2—Y3 extends very close indeed to 0 so she is on a near
collision course. (Incidentally we can get her course and speed

in the same way as with X, if we want: the figure shows them to be 007°/15 K.)   Obviously we must alter to keep clear of Y. Suppose we decide to alter to have a closest approach of 2 miles.   We put in Y4 (without waiting for her to get there) and draw the line Y4—A′ tangential to the 2-mile Range Ring and draw back from Y3 a line parallel to Y4—A′.   With S as centre and radius S—Y0 we draw an arc to cut this line at B. If we wish to maintain our speed and keep clear by altering course only (normally the best practice) the angle YO—S—B is the alteration to starboard we need.   This is, from the figure, 64°.   We should therefore alter to 060°+64°=124° and if we alter to this when Y reaches position Y4—*i.e.* 24 minutes after she was first seen at YO—she will pass clear at 2 miles distant.   If, for any reason, we prefer to maintain course and keep clear by reducing speed, the required alteration can be obtained by noting the point C where YO—S cuts Y3—B. The length S—Y0 represents 10 K and the length S—C represents the speed to which we should reduce to clear by the required 2 miles.   From the scale under the diagram this is seen to be substantially 6 K.

Close Quarters Situations.   At close quarters, where there is not time to plot, one has to put up with second best and con the ship as carefully as possible on the basis of the information afforded by the afterglow " tails."   These rearward extensions of targets which are moving in relation to own ship are of lengths roughly proportional to the speed of relative motion and extend in a direction opposite to that of the relative motion.

Fig. 57 shows a typical close quarters situation.   The Range Change Switch is at 3 miles (plus) and there are three Range Rings 1 mile apart.   Seven ships, 1X, 2X, 3X, 4X, 5X, 1Y, and 2Y are on the screen.   4X has no tail and therefore has no relative motion to own ship—*i.e.* her course and speed are the same as ours.   1X, 2X, 3X, and 5X have tails extending parallel to the Heading Marker and therefore are on the same course as ourselves or on the reciprocal course.   The long tail, extending away from own ship, of the ahead ship 1X, indicates that she is closing fast, which is consistent with her being on a reciprocal course.   The short tail, also extending away from own ship, of the ahead ship 2X, indicates that she is being slowly overtaken on our course and therefore being slowly closed by us.

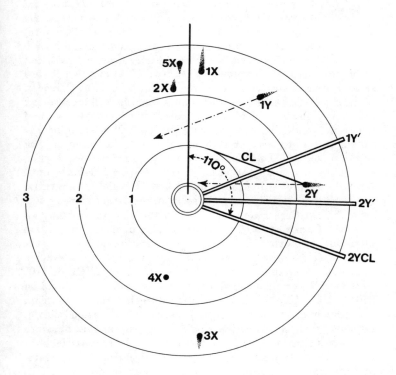

FIG. 57.

Similarly the short tail of the astern ship 3X indicates a slow closing movement, *i.e.* she is slowly overtaking us on our course. The short tail, extending towards own ship, of the ahead ship 5X indicates that she is pulling away ahead. None of the " X " ships is on a collision course and, apart from possible small alterations to obtain more comfortable separations when passing, no alterations are necessary.

Ships 1Y and 2Y, however, have tails the directions of which show that they are on courses closing our line of advance and either could be on a collision course. To test for this swing the Bearing Cursor (indicated by the double lines in the figure) parallel to each tail in turn, or use a straight edge along each tail, to estimate how near a forward prolongation of each tail comes to the screen centre. The type of Cursor which has several parallel lines is most convenient for this. The Cursor in position 1Y' for testing ship 1Y shows that she will cross ahead at a least distance of about 1¼ miles, which, in this sort of situation, would be regarded as adequate. But swinging the Cursor to 2Y' to test for ship 2Y, shows her to be on a near collision course. To clear her by a required distance—1 mile, say—alter course to starboard, or reduce speed, or both, until her tail is seen to swing round into a line CL which is tangential to the chosen (1 mile) Range Ring from the target " spot " 2Y, swinging the Cursor round parallel to this line and reading off from the Cursor scale the alteration angle necessary if you are intending to keep clear by course alteration alone. In the figure, which is drawn for course alteration alone, the alteration to starboard, as shown by the Cursor in position 2YCL, is 110° so that, if the original course was 060°, the new course would be 060°+110°. This is shown in the figure in order to explain the principles involved: in the particular situation shown, however, such an alteration would be highly inadvisable since it involves crossing ahead of the ship 1X. In this particularly awkward situation it would be best to clear ship 2Y by maintaining course, swinging the bearing Cursor to position 2YCL in which it is parallel to the line CL tangential to the 1 mile Range Ring from spot 2Y, and reducing speed until the tail from 2Y swings round into the line CL.

Radar in Restricted Channels. Underlying all the anti-collision radar navigation described above is the assumption that, until a specific alteration is made to keep clear of another ship, *all the ships concerned steer fixed compass courses at fixed speeds*. Of course this may not be possible, for obvious reasons, in the case of ships navigating in restricted channels and fairways. However, from a knowledge of your own heading and speed, and a knowledge of your own position along a channel, combined with a range and bearing taken of another ship and a study of the chart, it is usually easy to determine her position quickly and with sufficient accuracy to forecast her movements, and common sense will tell you what to do. In any case it is well to remember that most buoyed channels and fairways have depths in the channel for taking big ships of draught far exceeding your own, and that in the great majority of cases there is no God's reason why you should be in the channel at all. If you navigate just outside such channels you won't meet big ships, for they never go there. If you know what a 10 K tail looks like on your own radar (supposing you are a 10 K ship) it is not difficult to pick out the buoys on your screen—for they will all have 10 K tails as you approach them—and thus keep out of the way outside the buoys.

EPILOGUE

PERSONAL TO THE BEGINNER

Dear beginner, having borne with me so long, bear just a little longer. In your club, whichever it be, there is a sufficiency of grizzled amateur shell-backs who will tell you that many of the methods recommended here are " big ship " or " difficult "; that *they* first went to sea in the Ark (Captain Noah, Master); that they know every sandbank round our coasts and have been on most of them; and that, in all their centuries of experience, they have never found the need for an Admiralty Tide Table or an Admiralty Chart, or a Radar Plotting Sheet, while as for a sextant, well . . . !   Listen to these ancient mariners of the club bar with the respect their age deserves, for the beginner can always learn from the old hand, even if it is only what to avoid.   But keep in the back of your mind the fact that uninstructed experience may sometimes be no more than the repetition of one's own errors and prejudices, and do not, I beg of you, cut your cloths to their tailoring. Navigation, like other arts, depends for its quick and confident practice upon habit, and if you are starting from the beginning, it is as easy to acquire good habits as bad ones.   High among the bad ones is that of imagining that a radio direction finder provides an acceptable substitute for ordinary navigation methods and that all you have to do to keep out of trouble in mist or fog is merely to look at the "picture" on your radar screen.

And so: good ships, good sailing, and good luck.

ENGLAND, EAST COAST - WALTON ON THE NAZE

LAT 51°51'N   LONG 1°16'E

TIME ZONE GMT   TIMES AND HEIGHTS OF HIGH AND LOW WATERS

APRIL   MAY

```
      TIME   M   FT      TIME   M   FT       TIME   M   FT       TIME   M   FT       TIME   M   FT

    1 0304  0.8  2.6  16 0435  0.4  1.2    1 0319  0.5  1.5  16 0442  0.5  1.6    1 0441  0.4  1.?
      0932  3.7 12.2     1030  4.0 13.2      0948  4.1 13.6     1044  4.1 13.3      1101  4.3 14.
    F 1527  0.9  3.0  SA 1641  0.7  2.3   SU 1543  0.7  2.2   M 1652  0.6  2.0    W 1704  0.5  1
      2152  3.8 12.5     2242  4.0 13.0      2206  4.1 13.5     2259  4.0 13.1      2320  4.3  1

    2 0357  0.5  1.7  17 0513  0.4  1.2    2 0414  0.3  0.9  17 0515  0.5  1.7    2 0532  0.'
      1020  4.1 13.3     1111  4.1 13.5      1037  4.3 14.3     1122  4.1 13.5      1147  4.4
   SA 1616  0.7  2.2  SU 1718  0.6  1.9    M 1634  0.5  1.7   TU 1727  0.6  1.8   TH 1756  0.4
      2237  4.1 13.5     2323  4.1 13.4      2254  4.3 14.2     2337  4.0 13.2

    3 0447  0.3  1.0  18 0544  0.4  1.3    3 0505  0.2  0.7  18 0544  0.6  1.9    3 0008  4.4
      1104  4.3 14.2     1147  4.1 13.6      1122  4.5 14.7     1156  4.1 13.5      0619  0.4
   SU 1702  0.5  1.6  M  1750  0.5  1.7   TU 1722  0.4  1.4   W 1801  0.5  1.8    F 1232  4.
      2320  4.4 14.3     2359  4.1 13.5      2339  4.5 14.7                         1846  0

    4 0532  0.1  0.5  19 0612  0.4  1.5    4 0551  0.2  0.6  19 0012  4.0 13.2    4 0057  4.4
      1146  4.5 14.8     1221  4.2 13.6      1205  4.5 14.8     0612  0.6  2.1      0709  0.4
   M  1746  0.4  1.2  TU 1821  0.5  1.6    W 1808  0.4  1.2   TH 1228  4.1 13.4   SA 1319  4.
                                                               1832  0.6  1.9      1938

    5 0003  4.5 14.9  20 0035  4.1 13.6    5 0024  4.6 15.0  20 0045  4.0 13.1    5 0145  4.4
      0615  0.1  0.3     0639  0.5  1.7      0636  0.2  0.8     0642  0.7  2.3      075°
   TU 1228  4.6 15.0  W  1253  4.1 13.5   TH 1249  4.5 14.7   F 1259  4.1 13.3   SU 140°
      1827  0.3  1.1     1852  0.5  1.6      1856  0.3  1.1     1906  0.6  2.0      20?

    6 0043  4.6 15.2  21 0107  4.1 13.4    6 0110  4.6 15.0  21 0117  4.0 13.1    6 02
      0657  0.1  0.4     0723  0.6  1.9      0723  0.4  1.2     0714  0.8  2.6      08
   W  1309  4.5 14.9  TH 1323  4.1 13.4    F 1334  4.4 14.3   SA 1330  4.0 13.2    M 1°
      1909  0.4  1.2     1924  0.5  1.8      1945  0.4  1.3     1938  0.7  2.1      2°

    7 0126  4.6 15.1  22 0138  4.0 13.2    7 0158  4.5 14.7  22 0151  4.0 13.0    7 0°
      0740  0.3  0.9     0737  0.7  2.2      0811  0.6  1.8     0748  0.9  2.8      0'
   TH 1351  4.4 14.4  F  1352  4.0 13.1   SA 1419  4.2 13.8   SU 1404  4.0 13.1   TU 1
      1951  0.5  1.5     1957  0.6  2.1      2036  0.5  1.5     2013  0.7  2.3      2

    8 0209  4.5 14.7  23 0212  4.0 13.0    8 0247  4.3 14.1  23 0227  3.9 12.9    8 °
      0823  0.5  1.5     0811  0.8  2.6      0858  0.8  2.5     0822  0.9  3.1      '
    F 1434  4.2 13.8  SA 1425  3.9 12.9   SU 1505  4.0 13.1   M 1439  3.9 12.9    W
      2037  0.6  1.9     2032  0.7  2.4      2129  0.6  1.8     2050  0.7  2.4

    9 0257  4.3 14.0  24 0249  3.8 12.6    9 0339  4.1 13.3  24 0307  3.9 12.7    9
      0910  0.7  2.3     0847  0.9  3.1      0949  1.0  3.2     0858  1.0  3.3
   SA 1521  4.0 13.0  SU 1501  3.8 12.5    M 1556  3.8 12.5   TU 1518  3.8 12.6    °
      2131  0.7  2.3     2111  0.8  2.7      2227  0.7  2.1     2129  0.8  2.5

   10 0349  4.0 13.1  25 0328  3.7 12.1   10 0437  3.8 12.5  25 0350  3.8 12.°
      1004  0.9  3.1     0928  1.1  3.6      1045  1.1  3.7     0942  1.1  °
   SU 1613  3.7 12.2  M  1542  3.6 11.9   TU 1652  3.6 11.9   W 1603  3.7
      2234  0.8  2.6     2156  0.9  3.1      2330  0.7  2.3     2217  0

   11 0451  3.7 12.2  26 0416  3.5 11.6   11 0542  3.6 11.9  26 04'
      1108  1.1  3.6     1016  1.2  4.1      1149  1.2  3.9
   M  1715  3.5 11.5  TU 1631  3.5 11.4   W 1758  3.5 11.5
      2350  0.8  2.8     2249  1.0  3.3

   12 0605  3.5 11.6  27 0515  3.4 11.2   12 0041  0
      1219  1.2  3.9     1118  1.3  4.3      0655
   TU 1831  3.4 11.1  W  1734  3.3 11.0   TH 1°
                         2357  1.0  °

   13 0113  0.8  2.6  28 062°
      0728  3.5 11.5     1°
```

APPENDIX 1.

ENGLAND, EAST COAST

No.	PLACE	POSITION Lat. N.	POSITION Long. E.	HW 0000 and 1200	HW 0600 and 1800	LW 1100 and 2300	LW 0500 and 1700	MHWS	MHWN	MLWN	MLWS
129	**WALTON-ON-THE-NAZE** (STANDARD PORT)	(see page 52)						13·8	11·0	3·6	1·2
	SECONDARY PORTS			TIME DIFFERENCES (Zone G.M.T.)				HEIGHT DIFFERENCES			
121	Whitaker Beacon	51 40	1 06	+0022	+0024	+0027	+0033	+2·1	+1·7	+0·6	+0·3
	River Crouch										
121a	Holliwell Point	51 38	0 56	+0034	+0037	+0037	+0100	+3·7	+3·2	+0·9	+0·3
122	Burnham-on-Crouch	51 37	0 48	+0049	+0043	+0053	+0114	+4·1	+3·8	+1·0	+0·3
122a	Fenn Creek	51 38	0 36	+0130	+0110	◇	◇	◇	◇	◇	◇
	River Blackwater										
123	Bradwell-on-Sea	51 45	0 53	+0035	+0023	+0004	+0047	+3·5	+2·9	+0·8	+0·3
123a	Osea Island	51 43	0 46	+0057	+0045	+0007	+0050	+3·7	+3·2	+0·3	0·0
123b	Maldon	51 44	0 42	+0107	+0055	◇	◇	−4·2	−3·5	◇	◇
	River Colne										
126	Brightlingsea	51 48	1 00	+0025	+0021	+0004	+0046	+2·6	+1·6	+0·2	+0·2
126a	Wivenhoe	51 51	0 58	+0050	+0045	◇	◇	◇	◇	◇	◇
128	Clacton	51 47	1 09	+0012	+0110	+0008	+0025	+1·0	+0·6	0·0	+0·1
129	**WALTON-ON-THE-NAZE**	51 51	1 16	STANDARD PORT				See Table V			
130	Sunk Head Tower	51 46	1 30	0000	+0002	+0002	−0002	−0·9	−0·7	−0·2	−0·1

No.	PLACE	POSITION Lat. N.	POSITION Long. E.	HW 0000 and 1200	HW 0600 and 1800	LW 1100 and 2300	LW 0500 and 1700	MHWS	MHWN	MLWN	MLWS
129	**WALTON-ON-THE-NAZE** (STANDARD PORTS)	(see page 52)						4·2	3·4	1·1	0·4
	SECONDARY PORTS			TIME DIFFERENCES (Zone G.M.T.)				HEIGHT DIFFERENCES			
121	Whitaker Beacon	51 40	1 06	+0022	+0024	+0027	+0033	+0·6	+0·5	+0·2	+0·1
	River Crouch										
121a	Holliwell Point	51 38	0 56	+0034	+0037	+0037	+0100	+1·1	+0·9	+0·3	0·1
122	Burnham-on-Crouch	51 37	0 48	+0049	+0043	+0053	+0114	+1·3	+1·1	+0·3	+0·1
122a	Fenn Creek	51 38	0 36	+0130	+0110	◇	◇	◇	◇	◇	◇
	River Blackwater										
123	Bradwell-on-Sea	51 45	0 53	+0035	+0023	+0004	+0047	+1·1	+0·8	+0·2	+0·1
123a	Osea Island	51 43	0 46	+0057	+0045	+0007	+0050	+1·1	+0·9	+0·1	0·0
123b	Maldon	51 44	0 42	+0107	+0055	◇		−1·3	−1·1	◇	◆
	River Colne										
126	Brightlingsea	51 48	1 00	+0025	+0021	+0004	+0046	+0·8	+0·4	+0·1	0·0
126a	Wivenhoe	51 51	0 58	+0050	+0045	◇		◇		◇	◇
128	Clacton	51 47	1 09	+0012	+0010	+0008	+0025	+0·3	+0·1	0·0	0·0
129	**WALTON-ON-THE-NAZE**	51 51	1 16	STANDARD PORT				See Table V			
130	Sunk Head Tower	51 46	1 30	0000	+0002	+0002	−0002	−0·3	−0·3	−0·1	−0·1

APPENDIX 2.

WALTON ON THE NAZE
MEAN SPRING AND NEAP CURVES

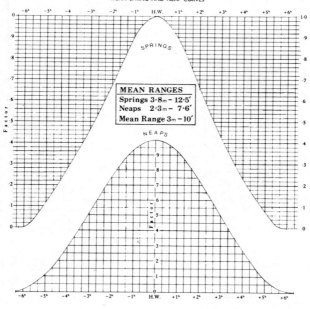

MEAN RANGES
Springs 3·8ₘ – 12·5′
Neaps   2·3ₘ – 7·6′
Mean Range 3ₘ – 10′

APPENDIX 3

DISTANCE BY CHANGE OF BEARING.

Change of Bearing	Angle from Bow at First Bearing.																		Change of Bearing
	20°	22°	24°	26°	28°	30°	32°	34°	36°	38°	40°	42°	44°	46°	48°	50°	52°	54°	
	Miles distant at Second Bearing for each mile of Run.																		
20	1·00	1·10	1·19	1·28	1·37	1·46	1·55	1·63	1·72	1·80	1·88	1·96	2·03	2·10	2·17	2·24	2·30	2·37	160
22	·91	1·00	1·09	1·17	1·25	1·34	1·41	1·49	1·57	1·64	1·72	1·79	1·85	1·92	1·98	2·04	2·10	2·16	158
24	·84	·92	1·00	1·08	1·15	1·23	1·30	1·37	1·45	1·51	1·58	1·65	1·71	1·77	1·83	1·88	1·94	1·99	156
26	·78	·85	·93	1·00	1·07	1·14	1·21	1·28	1·34	1·40	1·47	1·53	1·58	1·64	1·70	1·75	1·80	1·85	154
28	·73	·80	·87	·93	1·00	1·07	1·13	1·19	1·25	1·31	1·37	1·43	1·48	1·53	1·58	1·63	1·68	1·72	152
30	·68	·75	·81	·88	·94	1·00	1·06	1·12	1·18	1·23	1·29	1·34	1·39	1·44	1·49	1·53	1·58	1·62	150
32	·65	·71	·77	·83	·89	·94	1·00	1·06	1·11	1·16	1·21	1·26	1·31	1·36	1·40	1·45	1·49	1·53	148
34	·61	·67	·73	·78	·84	·89	·95	1·00	1·05	1·10	1·15	1·20	1·24	1·28	1·33	1·37	1·41	1·45	146
36	·58	·64	·69	·75	·80	·85	·90	·95	1·00	1·05	1·09	1·14	1·18	1·22	1·26	1·30	1·34	1·38	144
38	·56	·61	·66	·71	·76	·81	·86	·91	·95	1·00	1·04	1·09	1·13	1·17	1·21	1·24	1·28	1·31	142
40	·53	·58	·63	·68	·73	·78	·82	·87	·91	·96	1·00	1·04	1·08	1·12	1·16	1·19	1·23	1·26	140
42	·51	·56	·61	·66	·70	·75	·79	·84	·88	·92	·96	1·00	1·04	1·08	1·11	1·14	1·18	1·21	138
44	·49	·54	·59	·63	·68	·72	·76	·80	·85	·89	·93	·96	1·00	1·04	1·07	1·10	1·13	1·16	136
46	·48	·52	·57	·61	·65	·70	·74	·78	·82	·86	·89	·93	·97	1·00	1·03	1·06	1·09	1·12	134

APPENDIX 4.

MAST-HEAD ANGLES

Distance in Yards.	Height.								Distance in Yards.
	126 ft.	129 ft.	132 ft.	135 ft.	138 ft.	141 ft.	144 ft.	147 ft.	
2000	1 12·2	1 13·9	1 15·6	1 17·4	1 19·1	1 20·8	1 22·5	1 24·2	2000
2100	1 8·8	1 10·4	1 12·0	1 13·7	1 15·3	1 17·0	1 18·6	1 20·2	2100
2200	1 5·6	1 7·2	1 8·8	1 10·4	1 11·9	1 13·5	1 15·0	1 16·6	2200
2300	1 2·8	1 4·3	1 5·8	1 7·3	1 8·8	1 10·3	1 11·7	1 13·2	2300
2400	1 0·2	1 1·6	1 3·0	1 4·5	1 5·9	1 7·4	1 8·8	1 10·2	2400
2500	0 57·8	0 59·2	1 0·5	1 1·9	1 3·3	1 4·7	1 6·0	1 7·4	2500
2600	0 55·5	0 56·9	0 58·2	0 59·5	1 0·8	1 2·2	1 3·5	1 4·8	2600
2700	0 53·5	0 54·8	0 56·0	0 57·3	0 58·6	0 59·9	1 1·1	1 2·4	2700
2800	0 51·6	0 52·8	0 54·0	0 55·3	0 56·5	0 57·7	0 58·9	1 0·2	2800
2900	0 49·8	0 51·0	0 52·2	0 53·4	0 54·5	0 55·7	0 56·9	0 58·1	2900
3000	0 48·1	0 49·3	0 50·4	0 51·6	0 52·7	0 53·9	0 55·0	0 56·2	3000
3100	0 46·6	0 47·7	0 48·8	0 49·9	0 51·0	0 52·1	0 53·2	0 54·3	3100
3200	0 45·1	0 46·2	0 47·3	0 48·4	0 49·4	0 50·5	0 51·6	0 52·7	3200
3300	0 43·8	0 44·8	0 45·8	0 46·9	0 47·9	0 49·0	0 50·0	0 51·1	3300
3400	0 42·5	0 43·5	0 44·5	0 45·5	0 46·5	0 47·5	0 48·5	0 49·6	3400
3500	0 41·3	0 42·3	0 43·2	0 44·2	0 45·2	0 46·2	0 47·1	0 48·1	3500
3600	0 40·1	0 41·1	0 42·0	0 43·0	0 43·9	0 44·9	0 45·8	0 46·8	3600
3700	0 39·0	0 40·0	0 40·9	0 41·8	0 42·7	0 43·7	0 44·6	0 45·6	3700
3800	0 38·0	0 38·9	0 39·8	0 40·7	0 41·6	0 42·5	0 43·4	0 44·3	3800
3900	0 37·0	0 37·9	0 38·8	0 39·7	0 40·5	0 41·4	0 42·3	0 43·2	3900
4000	0 36·0	0 36·9	0 37·8	0 38·7	0 39·5	0 40·4	0 41·3	0 42·2	4000
4500	0 32·1	0 32·9	0 33·6	0 34·4	0 35·1	0 35·9	0 36·7	0 37·5	4500
5000	0 28·9	0 29·6	0 30·3	0 31·0	0 31·6	0 32·3	0 33·0	0 33·7	5000
5500	0 26·3	0 26·9	0 27·5	0 28·2	0 28·8	0 29·4	0 30·0	0 30·7	5500
6000	0 24·1	0 24·7	0 25·2	0 25·8	0 26·4	0 27·0	0 27·5	0 28·1	6000
6500	0 22·2	0 22·8	0 23·3	0 23·8	0 24·3	0 24·9	0 25·4	0 25·9	6500
7000	0 20·6	0 21·1	0 21·6	0 22·1	0 22·6	0 23·1	0 23·6	0 24·1	7000
7500	0 19·3	0 19·8	0 20·2	0 20·7	0 21·1	0 21·6	0 22·0	0 22·5	7500
8000	0 18·1	0 18·5	0 18·9	0 19·4	0 19·8	0 20·2	0 20·6	0 21·1	8000

APPENDIX 5.

Distance of the Sea Horizon.

Sea-Miles.

Note.—Abnormal Refraction may alter these values.

H'ght of Eye.	Dis-tance.	H'ght of Eye.	Dis-tance.	H'ght of Eye.	Dis-tance.	H'ght of Eye.	Dis-tance.
feet.	miles.	feet.	miles.	feet.	miles.	feet.	miles.
		50	8·12	100	11·5	200	16·2
1	1·15	51	8·20	102	11·6	210	16·6
2	1·62	52	8·28	104	11·7	220	17·0
3	1·99	53	8·36	106	11·8	230	17·4
4	2·30	54	8·44	108	11·9	240	17·8
5	2·57	55	8·52	110	12·0	250	18·2
6	2·81	56	8·59	112	12·1	260	18·5
7	3·04	57	8·67	114	12·3	270	18·9
8	3·25	58	8·74	116	12·4	280	19·2
9	3·44	59	8·82	118	12·5	290	19·6
10	3·63	60	8·89	120	12·6	300	19·9
11	3·81	61	8·97	122	12·7	310	20·2
12	3·98	62	9·03	124	12·8	320	20·5
13	4·14	63	9·11	126	12·9	330	20·9
14	4·30	64	9·19	128	13·0	340	21·2
15	4·45	65	9·26	130	13·1	350	21·5
16	4·59	66	9·33	132	13·2	360	21·8
17	4·73	67	9·40	134	13·3	370	22·1
18	4·87	68	9·47	136	13·4	380	22·4
19	5·00	69	9·54	138	13·5	390	22·7
20	5·13	70	9·61	140	13·6	400	23·0
21	5·26	71	9·67	142	13·7	420	23·5
22	5·39	72	9·74	144	13·8	440	24·1
23	5·51	73	9·81	146	13·9	460	24·6
24	5·62	74	9·88	148	14·0	480	25·2
25	5·74	75	9·94	150	14·1	500	25·7
26	5·85	76	10·01	152	14·2	520	26·2
27	5·97	77	10·07	154	14·2	540	26·7
28	6·08	78	10·14	156	14·3	560	27·2
29	6·18	79	10·20	158	14·4	580	27·7
30	6·29	80	10·27	160	14·5	600	28·1
31	6·39	81	10·33	162	14·6	620	28·6
32	6·50	82	10·40	164	14·7	640	29·0
33	6·60	83	10·46	166	14·8	660	29·5
34	6·69	84	10·52	168	14·9	680	29·9
35	6·79	85	10·59	170	15·0	700	30·4
36	6·89	86	10·65	172	15·1	720	30·8
37	6·98	87	10·71	174	15·1	740	31·2
38	7·08	88	10·77	176	15·2	760	31·7
39	7·17	89	10·83	178	15·3	780	32·1
40	7·26	90	10·89	180	15·4	800	32·5
41	7·35	91	10·95	182	15·5	820	32·9
42	7·44	92	11·01	184	15·6	840	33·3
43	7·53	93	11·07	186	15·6	860	33·7
44	7·62	94	11·13	188	15·7	880	34·1
45	7·70	95	11·19	190	15·8	900	34·4
46	7·79	96	11·25	192	15·9	920	34·8
47	7·87	97	11·31	194	16·0	940	35·2
48	7·95	98	11·37	196	16·1	960	35·6
49	8·04	99	11·42	198	16·2	980	35·9
50	8·12	100	11·48	200	16·2	1000	36·3

APPENDIX 6.

TRAVERSE TABLE.

Distance.	9		10		11		12		13		14		15		16		
CO.	Diff. LAT.	DEP.	Diff. LAT.	DEP.	Diff. LAT.	DEP.	Diff. LAT.	DEP.	Diff. LAT.	DEP.	Diff. LAT.	DEP.	Diff. LAT.	DEP.	Diff. LAT.	DEP.	CO.
	cos.	sin.	cos.	sin.	cos.	sin.	cos.	sin.	cos.	sin.	cos.	sin.	cos.	sin.	cos.	sin.	
1°	9·0	0·2	10·0	0·2	11·0	0·2	12·0	0·2	13·0	0·2	14·0	0·3	15·0	0·3	16·0	0·3	89°
2	9·0	0·3	10·0	0·3	11·0	0·4	12·0	0·4	13·0	0·5	14·0	0·5	15·0	0·5	16·0	0·6	88
3	9·0	0·5	10·0	0·5	11·0	0·6	12·0	0·6	13·0	0·7	14·0	0·7	15·0	0·8	16·0	0·8	87
4	9·0	0·6	10·0	0·7	11·0	0·8	12·0	0·8	13·0	0·9	14·0	1·0	15·0	1·0	16·0	1·1	86
5	9·0	0·8	10·0	0·9	11·0	1·0	12·0	1·0	13·0	1·1	13·9	1·2	14·9	1·3	15·9	1·4	85
6	9·0	0·9	9·9	1·0	10·9	1·1	11·9	1·3	12·9	1·4	13·9	1·5	14·9	1·6	15·9	1·7	84
7	8·9	1·1	9·9	1·2	10·9	1·3	11·9	1·5	12·9	1·6	13·9	1·7	14·9	1·8	15·9	1·9	83
8	8·9	1·3	9·9	1·4	10·9	1·5	11·9	1·7	12·9	1·8	13·9	1·9	14·9	2·1	15·8	2·2	82
9	8·9	1·4	9·9	1·6	10·9	1·7	11·9	1·9	12·8	2·0	13·8	2·2	14·8	2·3	15·8	2·5	81
10	8·9	1·6	9·8	1·7	10·8	1·9	11·8	2·1	12·8	2·3	13·8	2·4	14·8	2·6	15·8	2·8	80
11	8·8	1·7	9·8	1·9	10·8	2·1	11·8	2·3	12·8	2·5	13·7	2·7	14·7	2·9	15·7	3·1	79
12	8·8	1·9	9·8	2·1	10·8	2·3	11·7	2·5	12·7	2·7	13·7	2·9	14·7	3·1	15·7	3·3	78
13	8·8	2·0	9·7	2·2	10·7	2·5	11·7	2·7	12·7	2·9	13·6	3·1	14·6	3·4	15·6	3·6	77
14	8·7	2·2	9·7	2·4	10·7	2·7	11·6	2·9	12·6	3·1	13·6	3·4	14·6	3·6	15·5	3·9	76
15	8·7	2·3	9·7	2·6	10·6	2·8	11·6	3·1	12·6	3·4	13·5	3·6	14·5	3·9	15·5	4·1	75
16	8·7	2·5	9·6	2·8	10·6	3·0	11·5	3·3	12·5	3·6	13·5	3·9	14·4	4·1	15·4	4·4	74
17	8·6	2·6	9·6	2·9	10·5	3·2	11·5	3·5	12·4	3·8	13·4	4·1	14·3	4·4	15·3	4·7	73
18	8·6	2·8	9·5	3·1	10·5	3·4	11·4	3·7	12·4	4·0	13·3	4·3	14·3	4·6	15·2	4·9	72
19	8·5	2·9	9·5	3·3	10·4	3·6	11·3	3·9	12·3	4·2	13·2	4·6	14·2	4·9	15·1	5·2	71
20	8·5	3·1	9·4	3·4	10·3	3·8	11·3	4·1	12·2	4·4	13·2	4·8	14·1	5·1	15·0	5·5	70
21	8·4	3·2	9·3	3·6	10·3	3·9	11·2	4·3	12·1	4·7	13·1	5·0	14·0	5·4	14·9	5·7	69
22	8·3	3·4	9·3	3·7	10·2	4·1	11·1	4·5	12·1	4·9	13·0	5·2	13·9	5·6	14·8	6·0	68
23	8·3	3·5	9·2	3·9	10·1	4·3	11·0	4·7	12·0	5·1	12·9	5·5	13·8	5·9	14·7	6·3	67
24	8·2	3·7	9·1	4·1	10·0	4·5	11·0	4·9	11·9	5·3	12·8	5·7	13·7	6·1	14·6	6·5	66
25	8·2	3·8	9·1	4·2	10·0	4·6	10·9	5·1	11·8	5·5	12·7	5·9	13·6	6·3	14·5	6·8	65
26	8·1	3·9	9·0	4·4	9·9	4·8	10·8	5·3	11·7	5·7	12·6	6·1	13·5	6·6	14·4	7·0	64
27	8·0	4·1	8·9	4·5	9·8	5·0	10·7	5·4	11·6	5·9	12·5	6·4	13·4	6·8	14·3	7·3	63
28	7·9	4·2	8·8	4·7	9·7	5·2	10·6	5·6	11·5	6·1	12·4	6·6	13·2	7·0	14·1	7·5	62
29	7·9	4·4	8·7	4·8	9·6	5·3	10·5	5·8	11·4	6·3	12·2	6·8	13·1	7·3	14·0	7·8	61
30	7·8	4·5	8·7	5·0	9·5	5·5	10·4	6·0	11·3	6·5	12·1	7·0	13·0	7·5	13·9	8·0	60
31	7·7	4·6	8·6	5·2	9·4	5·7	10·3	6·2	11·1	6·7	12·0	7·2	12·9	7·7	13·7	8·2	59
32	7·6	4·8	8·5	5·3	9·3	5·8	10·2	6·4	11·0	6·9	11·9	7·4	12·7	7·9	13·6	8·5	58
33	7·5	4·9	8·4	5·4	9·2	6·0	10·1	6·5	10·9	7·1	11·7	7·6	12·6	8·2	13·4	8·7	57
34	7·5	5·0	8·3	5·6	9·1	6·2	9·9	6·7	10·8	7·3	11·6	7·8	12·4	8·4	13·3	8·9	56
35	7·4	5·2	8·2	5·7	9·0	6·3	9·8	6·9	10·6	7·5	11·5	8·0	12·3	8·6	13·1	9·2	55
36	7·3	5·3	8·1	5·9	8·9	6·5	9·7	7·1	10·5	7·6	11·3	8·2	12·1	8·8	12·9	9·4	54
37	7·2	5·4	8·0	6·0	8·8	6·6	9·6	7·2	10·4	7·8	11·2	8·4	12·0	9·0	12·8	9·6	53
38	7·1	5·5	7·9	6·2	8·7	6·8	9·5	7·4	10·2	8·0	11·0	8·6	11·8	9·2	12·6	9·9	52
39	7·0	5·7	7·8	6·3	8·5	6·9	9·3	7·6	10·1	8·2	10·9	8·8	11·7	9·4	12·4	10·1	51
40	6·9	5·8	7·7	6·4	8·4	7·1	9·2	7·7	10·0	8·4	10·7	9·0	11·5	9·6	12·3	10·3	50
41	6·8	5·9	7·5	6·6	8·3	7·2	9·1	7·9	9·8	8·5	10·6	9·2	11·3	9·8	12·1	10·5	49
42	6·7	6·0	7·4	6·7	8·2	7·4	8·9	8·0	9·7	8·7	10·4	9·4	11·1	10·0	11·9	10·7	48
43	6·6	6·1	7·3	6·8	8·0	7·5	8·8	8·2	9·5	8·9	10·2	9·5	11·0	10·2	11·7	10·9	47
44	6·5	6·3	7·2	6·9	7·9	7·6	8·6	8·3	9·4	9·0	10·1	9·7	10·8	10·4	11·5	11·1	46
45	6·4	6·4	7·1	7·1	7·8	7·8	8·5	8·5	9·2	9·2	9·9	9·9	10·6	10·6	11·3	11·3	45
	sin.	cos.	sin.	cos.	sin.	cos.	sin.	cos.	sin.	cos.	sin.	cos.	sin.	cos.	sin.	cos.	
CO.	DEP.	Diff. LAT.	DEP.	Diff. LAT.	DEP.	Diff. LAT.	DEP.	Diff. LAT	DEP.	Diff. LAT.	DEP.	Diff. LAT.	DEP.	Diff. LAT.	DEP.	Diff. LAT.	CO.

APPENDIX 7.

DEPARTURE into d. Longitude

Dep.	Middle Latitude										Dep.
	50°	51°	52°	53°	54°	55°	56°	57°	58°	59°	
	sec.	sec.	sec.	sec.	sec.	sec.	sec.	sec.	sec.	sec.	
1	1·6	1·6	1·6	1·7	1·7	1·7	1·8	1·8	1·9	1·9	1
2	3·1	3·2	3·2	3·3	3·4	3·5	3·6	3·7	3·8	3·9	2
3	4·7	4·8	4·9	5·0	5·1	5·2	5·4	5·5	5·7	5·8	3
4	6·2	6·4	6·5	6·6	6·8	7·0	7·2	7·3	7·5	7·8	4
5	7·8	7·9	8·1	8·3	8·5	8·7	8·9	9·2	9·4	9·7	5
6	9·3	9·5	9·7	10·0	10·2	10·5	10·7	11·0	11·3	11·6	6
7	10·9	11·1	11·4	11·6	11·9	12·2	12·5	12·9	13·2	13·6	7
8	12·4	12·7	13·0	13·3	13·6	13·9	14·3	14·7	15·1	15·5	8
9	14·0	14·3	14·6	15·0	15·3	15·7	16·1	16·5	17·0	17·5	9
10	15·6	15·9	16·2	16·6	17·0	17·4	17·9	18·4	18·9	19·4	10
11	17·1	17·5	17·9	18·3	18·7	19·2	19·7	20·2	20·8	21·4	11
12	18·7	19·1	19·5	19·9	20·4	20·9	21·5	22·0	22·6	23·3	12
13	20·2	20·7	21·1	21·6	22·1	22·7	23·2	23·9	24·5	25·2	13
14	21·8	22·2	22·7	23·3	23·8	24·4	25·0	25·7	26·4	27·2	14
15	23·3	23·8	24·4	24·9	25·5	26·2	26·8	27·5	28·3	29·1	15
16	24·9	25·4	26·0	26·6	27·2	27·9	28·6	29·4	30·2	31·1	16
17	26·4	27·0	27·5	28·2	28·9	29·6	30·4	31·2	32·1	33·0	17
18	28·0	28·6	29·2	29·9	30·6	31·4	32·2	33·0	34·0	34·9	18
19	29·6	30·2	30·9	31·6	32·3	33·1	34·0	34·9	35·9	36·9	19
20	31·1	31·8	32·5	33·2	34·0	34·9	35·8	36·7	37·7	38·8	20
21	32·7	33·4	34·1	34·9	35·7	36·6	37·6	38·6	39·6	40·8	21
22	34·2	35·0	35·7	36·6	37·4	38·4	39·3	40·4	41·5	42·7	22
23	35·8	36·5	37·4	38·2	39·1	40·1	41·1	42·2	43·4	44·7	23
24	37·3	38·1	39·0	39·9	40·8	41·8	42·9	44·1	45·3	46·6	24
25	38·9	39·7	40·6	41·5	42·5	43·6	44·7	45·9	47·2	48·5	25
26	40·4	41·3	42·2	43·2	44·2	45·3	46·5	47·7	49·1	50·5	26
27	42·0	42·9	43·9	44·9	45·9	47·1	48·3	49·6	51·0	52·4	27
28	43·6	44·5	45·5	46·5	47·6	48·8	50·1	51·4	52·8	54·4	28
29	45·1	46·1	47·1	48·2	49·3	50·6	51·9	53·2	54·7	56·3	29
30	46·7	47·7	48·7	49·3	51·0	52·3	53·6	55·1	56·6	58·2	30
31	48·2	49·3	50·4	51·5	52·7	54·0	55·4	56·9	58·5	60·2	31
32	49·8	50·8	52·0	53·2	54·4	55·8	57·2	58·8	60·4	62·1	32
33	51·3	52·4	53·6	54·8	56·1	57·5	59·0	60·6	62·3	64·1	33
34	52·9	54·0	55·2	56·5	57·8	59·3	60·8	62·4	64·2	66·0	34
35	54·4	55·6	56·8	58·2	59·5	61·0	62·6	64·3	66·0	68·0	35
36	56·0	57·2	58·5	59·8	61·2	62·8	64·4	66·1	67·9	69·9	36
37	57·6	58·8	60·1	61·5	62·9	64·5	66·2	67·9	69·8	71·8	37
38	59·1	60·4	61·7	63·1	64·6	66·3	68·0	69·8	71·7	73·8	38
39	60·7	62·0	63·3	64·8	66·3	68·0	69·7	71·6	73·6	75·7	39
40	62·2	63·6	65·0	66·5	68·1	69·7	71·5	73·4	75·5	77·7	40
41	63·8	65·2	66·6	68·1	69·8	71·5	73·3	75·3	77·4	79·6	41
42	65·3	66·7	68·2	69·8	71·5	73·2	75·1	77·1	79·3	81·5	42
43	66·9	68·3	69·8	71·5	73·2	75·0	76·9	79·0	81·1	83·5	43
44	68·5	69·9	71·5	73·1	74·9	76·7	78·7	80·8	83·0	85·4	44
45	70·0	71·5	73·1	74·8	76·6	78·5	80·5	82·6	84·9	87·4	45
46	71·6	73·1	74·7	76·4	78·3	80·2	82·3	84·5	86·8	89·3	46
47	73·1	74·7	76·3	78·1	80·0	81·9	84·0	86·3	88·7	91·3	47
48	74·7	76·3	78·0	79·8	81·7	83·7	85·8	88·1	90·6	93·2	48
49	76·2	77·9	79·6	81·4	83·4	85·4	87·6	90·0	92·5	95·1	49
50	77·8	79·5	81·2	83·1	85·1	87·2	89·4	91·8	94·4	97·1	50
	cosec.	cosec.	cosec.	cosec.	cosec.	cosec.	cosec.	cosec.	cosec.	cosec.	
	40°	39°	38°	37°	36°	35°	34°	33°	32°	31°	

d. Long. = Dep. × Sec. Mid-Lat.

APPENDIX 8.

COMPASS CONVERSION TABLE

Circular	Quadrantal	Points	Circular	Quadrantal	Points
000	N	N	180	S	S
011¼	N 11¼ E	N × E	191¼	S 11¼ W	S × W
022½	N 22½ E	NNE	202½	S 22½ W	SSW
033¾	N 33¾ E	NE × N	213¾	S 33¾ W	SW × S
045	N 45 E	NE	225	S 45 W	SW
056¼	N 56¼ E	NE × E	236¼	S 56¼ W	SW × W
067½	N 67½ E	ENE	247½	S 67½ W	WSW
078¾	N 78¾ E	E × N	258¾	S 78¾ W	W × S
090	E	E	270	W	W
101¼	S 78¾ E	E × S	281¼	N 78¾ W	W × N
112½	S 67½ E	ESE	292½	N 67½ W	WNW
123¾	S 56¼ E	SE × E	303¾	N 56¼ W	NW × W
135	S 45 E	SE	315	N 45 W	NW
146¼	S 33¾ E	SE × S	326¼	N 33¾ W	NW × N
157½	S 22½ E	SSE	337½	N 22½ W	NNW
168¾	S 11¼ E	S × E	348¾	N 11¼ W	N × W
180	S	S	360	N	N

INDEX